Gail has de-mystified neuroscience enhancing leadership ability. Throug exercises, she takes the reader on a jo and motivation. Essential knowledge and skills for all leaders in developing high performance teams.

Honourable Susan Lenehan, Board Chairman, former CEO and Government Minister

Gail explains the latest knowledge from psychology and neuroscience providing executive leaders with powerful tools for managing their own behaviours and understanding the behaviours of others.

Jon Isaacs, Fellow of the Australian Institute of Company Directors (over 17 years as a professional Executive Coach and Mentor)

This book is practical and focused. What is particularly helpful is the structured approach, brief organised chapters and 'real world' examples. I found the tools for understanding ourselves and our environment helpful and challenging. I got more 'now I understand moments' reading this small volume of condensed wisdom than any other book in many years. A definite read.

Shaun Browne, Director and CEO of AME Group

This is an essential book for us all, particularly those involved in the coaching world. It reminds us that to succeed we must manage our thoughts. This book leaves me feeling joy as we can learn from the insights of modern research and use new skills for leadership, without an MBA.

Phillip Hart, Director Phillip Hart Consulting, Master Coach, Mentor, Facilitator

As an avid reader of leadership literature, I sometimes despair at the 'impracticality' of some books. *The Brain's Business* is different in that it contains plenty of tips and tools that a busy leader can apply in all aspects of their life.

Ian Schubach, Co-Founder Peak Teams

The Brain's Business brings to life the ever-increasing research on the importance of our brain and its plasticity to leadership. Thank you, Gail.

Dr Lana Ledgerwood, Cognitive Neuroscientist and Leadership Consultant

For my husband Jon who was so important in creating the vision behind this book, for his practical help, encouragement and enduring love

The Brain's Business

The Brain's Business

Psychology & Neuroscience

For Exceptional Leadership

Gail Pemberton

National Library of Australia Cataloguing-in-Publication entry

Creator:	Pemberton, Gail (Gail Marie Russell), 1950– author.
Title:	The brain's business : psychology & neuroscience for exceptional leadership / Gail Pemberton.
ISBN:	9780994469700 (paperback)
Subjects:	Leadership—Psychological aspects. Unconscious. Emotional intelligence.

Dewey Number: 658.4092

For further information please contact www.buythatbook.com.au

Cover photo by Saad Faruque
Cover design by Caroline Pemberton and Rodriguo Adolfo
Printed in Australia by Ingram Spark

Contents

Acknowledgements

There are so many invaluable people to acknowledge for helping me bring this book to fruition. Some of the most important are the hundreds of clients I have worked with over the years. Without them I could not have developed and honed the knowledge I bring to you here. I have often thought that perhaps I should be paying them for their time rather than being paid! But that would be a terrible business model, as after all, this book is about psychology and business.

I showed the first draft to Dr Lana Ledgerwood, cognitive neuroscientist and leadership consultant. Her encouragement and comments were so important to me.

Denise Weinreis, Adjunct Associate Professor at the Australian Graduate School of Management at the UNSW School of Business went through the manuscript with a fine toothcomb for which I will be forever grateful.

Dr Sally White, an organisational psychologist, adjunct faculty at the Australian Graduate School of Management also vetted it for accuracy and offered encouragement.

My daughter Caroline who helped me loosen up my style and made some important suggestions, and my husband Jon who helped me write the corporate program, which this book is based on. Many people gave me great suggestions such as Julian Fairfield of Bach Consulting, Wes Tobin from Westpac, and many of the people who have actually endorsed the book with their recommendations. Noelene Lowes who typeset this book, Isabelle Fogarty who did a magnificent job proofreading and Saad Faruque for his brilliant design of the brain shown on the cover.

To you all I owe a big debt of gratitude, thank you.

Introduction

> **Our brains are up to more than we think and they are impacting our bottom line**

There's a large part of your brain, your unconscious, yes you read that right, your unconscious that influences all your behaviour, beliefs and thoughts, yet we are largely unaware of its presence let alone its power. It impacts every emotion we have and fuels our every motivation. Few of us even know about it, yet there it is working away in everyone's brain.

This hidden part of the brain affects everything in business, from the bottom line to workplace efficiency, productivity, resilience and staff turnover, because a successful business is its people.

If we want a competitive edge it is now available for the taking. We've reaped the rewards of better processes, technology and faster communications but it's time to truly understand the 'people' at the heart of business and unlock further potential. While we know that a company's value depends on its people we don't really know how to harness further value. We put our staff through numerous expensive training programs and all are useful to some degree, yet we seem to skip the basics of what drives each and every individual and how that impacts on their emotional well-being and subsequent productivity.

1

This understanding is particularly relevant, as the Gen X and Y employees expect more than their predecessors. They want to develop personally with freedom, independence, diversity and change. These generations are our future leaders and their role is, and will be, to continue to raise the level of consciousness. Goffee and Jones, in their article 'Why Should Anyone Be Led by You?'[1] say: "in these 'empowered' times followers are hard to find – except by leaders who excel at capturing people's hearts, minds and spirits". Many want to be leaders but you can't do anything in business without followers and Gen X and Y generally don't see themselves as followers. Social media has made them the conductors of their lives. As Goffee and Jones go on to say, many executives don't have the self-knowledge or the authenticity necessary for leadership that will capture people's hearts, minds and spirits to initially become followers.

The challenge is how do leaders get the self-knowledge and authenticity to lead? This is not easy, but it becomes easier when you know what to look for and become aware of what drives you. What drives you also drives others so when you truly know yourself it becomes much easier to know others and how to motivate them. This journey starts with you.

I suspect that if you were asked to draw two circles, one circle to represent all that you have achieved, your educational achievements, your status within the organisation, your wealth etc, and the second circle to

---

[1] Professors Robert Goffee and Gareth Jones, 'Why Should Anyone be Led by You?', *Harvard Business Review*, On Point Article, Sept./Oct. 2000.

represent the amount of work you have done on growing your internal self, one circle would be much bigger than the other.

I imagine the biggest circle would symbolise what society holds dear and signifies success, your position and your wealth and what you want the external world to see.

The second circle you could call your EQ, emotional intelligence. It is harder to develop than your IQ. EQ is the time spent in self-reflection, in becoming aware of what drives you, in growing your own authenticity and internal ability to gauge external events. Consciously valuing and appreciating ourselves, is much more difficult for us than attaining the next promotion, surprising though that may sound. Unless we can appreciate ourselves and our needs it is difficult to truly appreciate others and their needs. Until we grow this second circle we may never realise our full potential to be the best leader that we can be.

Your internal journey

Your expertise, wealth, status, position as a leader, position within your organisation etc

What I would like to enable is to get your two circles looking more equal. These synergies then facilitate your full potential.

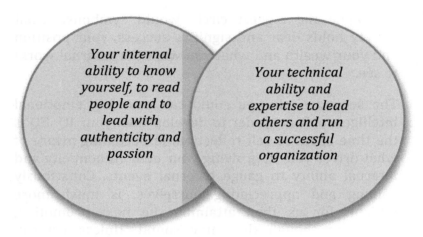

Your internal ability to know yourself, to read people and to lead with authenticity and passion

Your technical ability and expertise to lead others and run a successful organization

In order for you, your team and your company to move forward and sustain improvement we need to go back to the beginning. That beginning is a better understanding of human behaviour – why we think and react the way we do. This is the vital step that, most training programs miss, and hence the learning from these programs is not sustained because we soon default back to our original programming.

This book deals with hard facts, proven psychological principles, underpinned by neuroscience and how that knowledge impacts the corporate environment.

We are in the age of brain science. It is a unique theoretical era of change that could be likened to the advent of the printing press or the dawn of computerisation. Modern science using brain imaging techniques, now reveals a lot more about the brain's workings. Up until recently the brain was virtually ignored because we simply didn't know how it worked. My experience over 20 years has given me an insight into how this brain science impacts every aspect of your life, from your relationships, your business to everything you do.

In *The Brain's Business* I will show you the 7 keys to successful relationships, how the neuroscience fits and how you can harness cutting edge information to grow your business, your career and, most importantly, yourself. We will also cover the systems underpinning all organisations, corporate and social, and how they work.

The seven understandings will in turn cover:

- How extraordinary your brain is – the power of your unconscious

- How your brain was and continues to be programmed

- How it can sabotage you without you even realising it – until later

- How to work more efficiently in your business with the resultant impact on relationships, teamwork, productivity and profitability

- Most importantly, how you will achieve personal excellence

Over the years many clients have said "I wish I had known this earlier. It would have made such a difference to how I handled some difficult situations that I know have impacted my career and my advancement."

While much of the information in this short book is distilled from my earlier book, **You Can Live with Anyone, well almost**, which evolved from many years of practical experience, dealing with thousands of people from heads of industry to people mandated by the courts, **The Brain's Business** focuses on the nuances of business.

Psychotherapy was my second career, actually my third if I count motherhood.

I started work in a large London investment bank, with private clients' portfolios. When I moved to South Africa for five years I became a financial journalist and later returned to the banking industry there. In Australia I became a mother and later a psychotherapist. I had realised that the people running successful listed companies had an innate management skill in understanding what made their employees tick and how to motivate them. I wanted to understand that skill and how they acquired it. It was relatively easy to identify which companies would be successful after talking to their CEOs or CFOs and which I could recommend, either in my capacity as a journalist or as an investment analyst. Today I bridge both business and psychology, because I believe that if people have this brain/psychological knowledge it's invaluable.

Our issues and needs boil down to being very similar whether we are the head of a top 100 listed company or somebody coming out of jail. We need food, shelter, and we received programming from our parents or caregivers as children. This programming forms the basis of our beliefs and perceptions about the world and ourselves. From there we go on to have relationships and this is usually where the difficulties start. Underlying all human interactions are 7 key psychological understandings and once we have a handle on these, change begins. You will understand how you can make conscious choices moving forward. Believe it or not, while we may think we are in control most of the time we are not, and I'll show you why.

This work will improve your relationships and as Dr Louis Cozolino says in his book, *The Healthy Aging Brain*,[2] how well we age depends on the quality of our relationships. When you think of the amount of time you spend at work interacting with others it pays to make those relationships easier, more effective and stimulating. Dr Dan Siegel another expert neuroscientist, says: "our behaviour impacts our brain physiology. We know that experiences shape the brain throughout life by altering the connections among neurons".[3] This work changes your brain.

"Moment to moment our choices change the functioning of our brain and impacts the way we see the world and

---

[2] Dr Louis Cozolino, *The Healthy Aging Brain* (Professor, Department of Psychiatry and Behavioural Science, University of Washington, School of Medicine).

[3] Dr Dan Siegel, *Pocket Guide to Interpersonal Neurobiology* (Clinical Professor at UCLA School of Medicine).

interact with it," says Dr David Rock, one of the thought leaders in human performance.[4] With all the experts effectively saying the same thing it behoves us to look at this cutting edge information and be early adopters. The result will be improved productivity.

Here is a brief look at the vital 7 steps that form the foundation of this book and that will yield tangible results, for you and your company.

7 Keys

1. All our behaviour is initially motivated by 3Ss: Survival, Safety, and Security (crocodile brain).

2. Our instinctive drive to protect ourselves often causes emotional reactivity and destructive patterns in our relationships.

3. Our thinking patterns and behaviour today remain largely untouched since programming was laid down in early childhood.

4. This programming went into the unconscious and we do not realise that our unconscious influences our every thought and action.

   (Do you remember learning to drive? There was a lot to master, but now driving is second nature, you don't even think about it, you just do it. Our behaviour, attitude and thinking is also like this, embedded into our unconscious.)

---

[4] Jeff Schwartz, talking to Dr David Rock about 'Managing with the Brain in Mind'.

5. Our programming taught us to hide what was considered unacceptable behaviour and it sunk into our unconscious (cognitive dissonance).

6. To avoid looking at our own less than perfect characteristics we focus on others' faults – PROJECTION.

7. Our projections influence the way we think about others and that in turn affects our behaviour.

Throughout the book there are numerous examples to illustrate each of the keys. At the end of the book are two appendices that look at the 7 keys to empowerment and how the principles fit into the macro picture of our interactive behaviour.

(As a quick aside, I use the words: corporate, business, company, organisation interchangeably but all mean a collection of people working together to forge a profitable enterprise.)

At the end of each chapter I suggest a couple of exercises that will help you in your journey and you would find it helpful to make a note of what springs to mind, so as you progress through the book your journey unfolds more fully. (Perhaps use a separate exercise book for these.)

Chapter 1

The unacknowledged systems underlying business that can cause havoc

Let's briefly look at the business world we work in. Ideally this is where all the elements want to be working productively. When a part of the system doesn't work well the whole system is affected. For example: of all the parts making up a car if just the spark plugs don't work the car won't start. Business is not very different. If one part is not being productive it impacts the whole.

Although not generally acknowledged, the overarching structure for all business is made up of two different systems - a corporate system that is product orientated and a social system that is people orientated. Each one has differing fundamental needs. Conflict and loss of productivity arise when these two systems clash because employer/employee expectations are not being met.

Before we can make an improvement in organisational effectiveness it is important that these differences are understood. The table below outlines some of these differences.

Before a change in organisational effectiveness is possible these differences must be understood

Corporate System

Product oriented

It is competitive and to flourish needs to be flexible and adaptable

It is a rational system

Management's productivity is measured and accountable

Social System

People oriented

Even though we are at work we have human needs, which are emotional (backed by neuroscience)

Until people become aware of their needs and how they are trying to get them met their thinking is often inflexible and rigid

Human potential and goals are fulfilled when we are operating in alignment with our core needs

In an ideal business world, organisations would all generate profit and everyone employed would have the business's needs at the top of their list of priorities.

Ideally the corporate system, which is product and profitability focused, would govern the social system, the people part. The difficult news for business is that the underlying reality is very different. Management doesn't like to think that profitability is largely dependent on people, since managing people, with all their variables, makes business more difficult. When these systems clash, trouble begins.

Clashing systems

Corporate system   Social system

Most corporations think rationally in order to generate maximum profitability and this often ignores the emotional needs of its people. The bad news is that if the emotive aspect is ignored for too long employee enthusiasm and passion is steadily eroded. It is replaced by resentment because largely unmet social needs want to be heard and better still satisfied.

Rationality underlies most workplace agreements and consequently their success is often limited, particularly if people feel unheard, unsupported and undervalued. When resentment starts to rise it becomes a largely unspoken, unacknowledged de-motivator, which then rears its head in unhealthy work politics and a subsequent decline in productivity.

The needs of both systems have to be examined and this is where Abraham Maslow's[5] work is helpful. Maslow was a brilliant psychological expert on individual human needs and even though he developed his theory in 1954 it is relevant today. Maslow realised that there is a hierarchy of needs that must be met in order for individuals to operate at higher levels, i.e. the levels that corporations must operate at to be competitive in today's market.

Let's look briefly at Maslow's Hierarchy of Needs. His theory is that each individual's needs must be satisfied at the lower levels before they progress to the higher more complex levels. (Further on in the 7 keys I will talk about the lowest physical survival needs as the 3Ss, the prime fundamental motivators for all human behaviour. Survival, safety and security in that order.) We need to feel our world is organised, predictable, safe and stable.

Maslow says that when low level needs are satisfied they no longer drive us. If we have food and shelter we take that for granted and work hard to become safe and secure. Those needs met we want friends, mate etc. We want to feel we belong and are loved. When we have that in place we want to be respected and recognised so that our self-esteem can grow. Usually that comes from a feeling of personal achievement, competence and independence. The final crowning of our human journey is when we feel we have 'self-actualised', which means we have become the very best of who we are.

---

[5] Source: Dr Abraham Maslow (*Motivation and Personality*, New York, Harper and Row, 1954).

Maslow's Hierarchy of Needs

We also need to recognise that corporations have a hierarchy of needs and Maslow's approach can be adapted to illustrate these, as seen in the following table.

- Corporations need to maintain profitability to ensure ongoing operation so this is the survival level.

- The next level is for the corporation to feel the world is organised and predictable so that there is a platform for growth and continued profitability. (No organisation is safe if it finds itself in the middle of a war zone, unless of course it has been set up to profit from war.)

- The third level need for a corporation to prosper is a strong cohesive culture, evidenced by employees high morale and sense of well-being.

- The fourth level is to be seen as a leader, successful in the marketplace with expanding share and highly respected brands.

- The final attainment is for the corporation to fully use its unique potential for the benefit of shareholders and the community.

When we look at these two diagrams we can see there are many areas of overlapping interest. We each need to survive at the base level. Then both the corporation and employees, as individuals, need stability. For individuals that translates as our security, our superannuation fund or our assets, however the person may define these. The corporation needs a cohesive culture, which translates for employees as belonging; we need the corporation to help give us that. We feel we belong when we are part of a team. Our self-actualisation as individuals and the corporation's realisation of true potential fits nicely as the individual seeks to grow and enhance the corporation and the corporation seeks to help grow the employees' skills and talents.

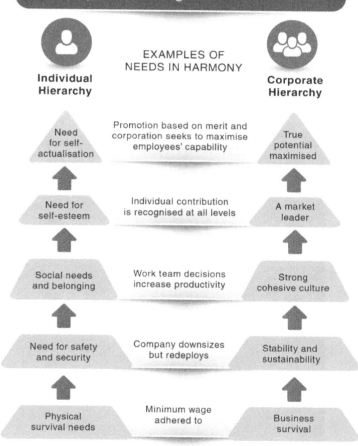

So that is the rosy picture. Now for the not so rosy picture when the two opposing pyramids of needs conflict for business reasons.

The hierarchical needs of the corporation and the individual can often conflict

EXAMPLE OF AREAS OF CONFLICT

Individual Hierarchy

Corporate Hierarchy

Individual Hierarchy	Example of areas of conflict	Corporate Hierarchy
Need for self-actualisation	Company depends on compeition between capable individuals — not all of us get promotion	True potential maximised
Need for self-esteem	Company may need to employ people where there is little scope for differentiation	A market leader
Social needs and belonging	Company wants flexibility unconstrained by collective action	Strong cohesive culture
Need for safety and security	Company may need to downsize — who goes?	Stability and sustainability
Physical survival needs	Employees might be exploited and underpaid	Business survival

The disappointing news for businesses is that, although the business objectives are of paramount importance, because organisations consist of people the social system will be more powerful. The conflict is that the social system works at a covert level and unless people's core needs are met business will not survive in the longer term.

Individuals will go to extraordinary lengths to satisfy their core needs and conflict occurs until these are met, as you can see in the next diagram.

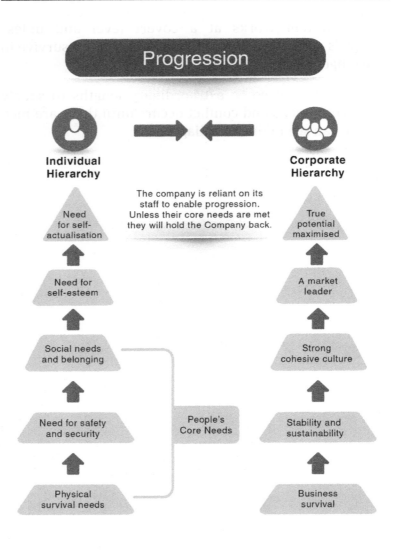

It is vital that management recognise the two different systems at play in business.

Management bridging the gap

Corporate System

Social System

Product oriented

People oriented

It is competitive and to flourish needs to be flexible and adaptable

Even though we are at work we have human needs, which are emotional (backed by neuroscience)

It is a rational system

Until people become aware of their needs and how they are trying to get them met their thinking is often inflexible and rigid

Management's productivity is measured and accountable

Human potential and goals are fulfilled when we are operating in alignment with our core needs

Ultimately people power will win out, as history has shown us over and over again – from the French Revolution to the fall of the Berlin wall and the disintegration of the USSR. However perhaps the greatest illustration in the business sense is the rise of the trade union movement; although when the workforce does not take into account the business's needs it will inevitably be laid off, as no business survives without profitability.

That said, leaders taking us into the next era of leadership will want to incorporate key psychological understandings into their management practice so there is less conflict between the political and social system. This will facilitate more self-sustaining businesses.

However this change doesn't happen without some disruption, as most of us prefer to stay the way we are rather than change. Unfortunately it is generally only conflict that precipitates change. In an organisational sense change becomes easier when it is initiated and implemented by everyone together.

The next part of understanding the systems that operate in business is called the theory of complexity. Complexity theory has been used in strategic management and is made up of a natural set of principles moving from chaos to rigidity.

It helps us to understand how organisations adapt to their environments and how they cope with situations of uncertainty.[6]

Mathematicians tell us that a complex system moving towards ever-increasing complexity brings stability. The important aspect here is if it is not allowed to move towards complexity it moves either towards chaos or rigidity. While business is already complex and many of us would like to simplify it, we cannot turn the clock back. We have to continue to move forward to stability, as obviously we don't want either rigidity or chaos.

It may seem a paradox yet for advancement it seems we need to continuously learn to operate in an ever more complex environment. This applies both at a personal level, a career level and for a business. We want people to be capable of self-organisation and we know that neither chaos nor rigidity is effective in today's business environment. The best part of this mathematical principle of complexity is that when a system is allowed to move towards complexity, with all the components being differentiated – ie, they are able to be different and separate, yet linked – then they operate as a functional whole in an optimal manner. It seems a contradiction but when a system moves towards complexity it is at its most flexible, adaptive and stable.[7]

---

[6] Professor Eve Mitleton-Kelly, Director Complexity Research Programme, London School of Economics, Ten Principles of Complexity & Enabling Infrastructures.

[7] Dr Dan J Siegel, *Parenting from the Inside Out.*

Complexity theory dictates that an organisation must aspire to and achieve higher and higher levels of complexity — or regression will occur

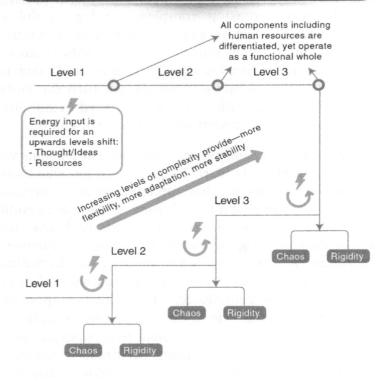

The complication is that if a system is not given the energy input to ascend to a level of complexity it will regress to either chaos or rigidity

The whole point of talking about the theory of complexity is when managers can guide business in ever more complex conditions without becoming rigid and without allowing it to become chaotic, it will flourish, as long as its people are encouraged to become differentiated.

Now to **differentiation** ... what is it?

To be differentiated is to be different and separate, ie, able to think for ourselves and be true to ourselves, yet be linked into the greater system.

We know that we are interdependent beings and want to be socially involved. We saw that in Maslow's Hierarchy of Needs, yet we also have an innate drive to be ourselves and to advance ourselves. If we can be taught to become more aware of our own programming (much more about programming in chapter 4) whilst recognising that others have their own programming as well, we can become less emotionally volatile. This in turn allows us a greater awareness of our behaviour and thoughts, as well as that of others. The result is that we are much more able to reach our potential as individuals within the confines of the system. We become more understanding while at the same time becoming differentiated – separate yet linked. This way we become less likely to be enmeshed in the politics of the organisation. The following diagrams from Otto Scharmer, the renowned American economist working from Massachusetts Institute of Technology and the author of Theory U, show this quite clearly.[8]

---

[8] Dr Otto Scharmer, *Theory U, Leading from the future as it emerges*, 2007.

To achieve differentiation of self, most individuals will need to go through a U shaped curve - this leads to awareness

Realised Self-Development

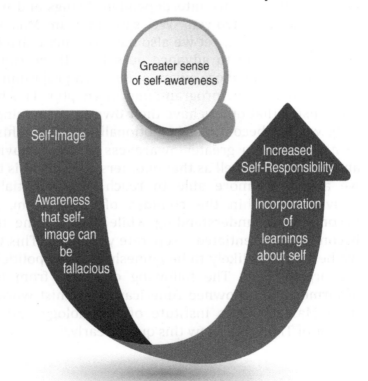

Greater sense of self-awareness

Self-Image

Increased Self-Responsibility

Awareness that self-image can be fallacious

Incorporation of learnings about self

The realisation that others are in the same boat

You can see from the following diagram how companies will benefit as individuals work at a new level of differentiation. (3Ss are covered in the next chapter.)

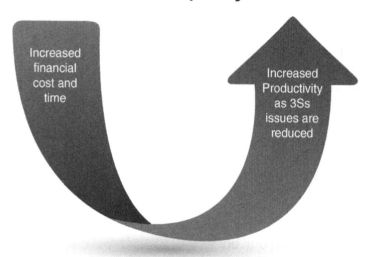

Although an initial cost is involved, when employees achieve awareness the company benefits as individuals are working at a new level of self-differentiation

Realised Company Benefits

Increased financial cost and time

Increased Productivity as 3Ss issues are reduced

Ongoing interest to facilitate long-term change

Before we turn our attention to the more personal side of the journey there is one more fundamental system at play in business, which is often overlooked and again comes back to managing people successfully.

We all know business works as a hierarchy, with the Board and CEO at the top and management and workers fanning out below. What we don't often realise is that at a subtle covert level the hierarchy of a business resembles the first hierarchy we were ever exposed to and that was the hierarchy in the family system.

In the traditional system Dad ostensibly ruled and Mum sat below him, perhaps the equivalent of Dad as Chairman and Mum as CEO. In a particularly equitable household perhaps Dad and Mum both sat at the top and children fanned out below them with the eldest also being co-opted into bringing the younger children in line. Generally speaking children were 'ordered around' and 'made' to do their parents' bidding. This system was unconsciously imprinted on us (more of this in chapters 3 and 4.) Today we, usually unconsciously, choose to obey those higher up the pecking order. The end result of this is that at an unconscious level we tend to look at our boss as either Mum or Dad.

Let's look at what an ideal, mythical Mum and Dad would look like and see if we unconsciously impose the same ideals on our boss.

Ideal parents will love us, forgive us our mistakes – even better, not see any – be encouraging, caring, gentle and kind as well as working hard to give us what we want. Let's be honest, isn't that what we would fantasize an ideal boss to be like? Except perhaps for the love bit; we could replace that with respect. Rationally we know it's an unrealistic picture, and the sad thing is that even now, at an unconscious level, that is what we would like to receive from our parents and often continue to try and achieve.

Let's look at where this can get us all into trouble now and you will see where problems arise.

As an employee, you have an unconscious need to be looked after and nurtured. Totally out of awareness you overlay the expectations of the idealised parent onto the boss. You want your boss to appreciate you, teach you, encourage you and praise you ... Does that resonate with some truth?

As a boss, with deadlines to meet, you want the work done efficiently and well, with as little hassle as possible. You pay your people a salary and expect good results without having to coach them every step of the way and without office politics and resentment rearing its head. As boss you rationally argue that your employees are not your children, they need to deliver and not whine behind the scenes because they want more of your attention and praise. Seems reasonable enough ...

The reality for management is that we all want appreciation and recognition. Pay is not enough.

Chapter Recap

In any business there are a number of systems in play, which are out of conscious awareness.

The primary systems are the corporate (which is interested in process, productivity and the bottom line) and the social system (people – and their needs).

Fundamentally this leads to a conflict of interest. People want their needs met and this may not correspond to a business's objectives.

Both business and people have fundamental needs that must be catered for (Maslow's hierarchy of needs) in order for each to be successful.

As business and people in today's age become more complex they can become more stable if they can adapt and become more flexible, rather than resisting change which leads to chaos and rigidity. However human nature wants homeostasis and not change. Change is unsettling.

Another system at work is the unconscious need of employees to think of the corporation as surrogate parents, there to encourage and keep everyone safe, which is not conducive to maximum productivity.

The desired outcome is differentiation when people can work within the system, be linked yet enabled to be creative and separate. This happens when employees feel secure within the system and have self-awareness. This facilitates greater productivity with reduced organisational politics.

Your journey

(In your exercise book record what comes up as you answer these questions. It will help you in the later chapters as you reflect on your own programming and beliefs.)

In your day-to-day interactions become aware of what systems you notice.

Observe your own dissatisfaction with authority figures within your organisation.

Describe what that dissatisfaction is about.

Chapter 2

**Your hidden brain, neuroscience and the first key
– All our behaviour is initially motivated by 3Ss:
Survival, Safety, and Security (crocodile brain).**

The 3Ss

What is this hidden part of the brain? Extraordinary as it
may seem it's our unconscious. So if it is unconscious
how is that going to help me to improve productivity in
my business and maximise my career success?

Great question! As I have said before, we are all human
and business is but a collection of individuals trying to
move forward. If we truly understand how individuals
work, functioning in a business becomes easier. But it
starts with you and understanding yourself. Let's take a
quick look at the neuroscience and how our brains are
wired.

Simple Neuroscience

The newest part of our brain the neo-cortex, the rational part

The second oldest part of the brain - the mammalian brain, the emotional part of unconscious

The oldest part of the brain - the reptilian brain, also part of unconscious

It is a bit frightening looking at the makeup of our brain as a series of cartoons, particularly the horse and the crocodile, but our whizz-bang, modern day brain actually developed and evolved in three stages. As it evolved, it tacked on new exciting bits capable of higher functioning, but never cleared out the older pre-programmed hardware and this has a nasty habit of sabotaging our more evolved neo-cortex. Think of it like a computer – the hardware is the same and we keep upgrading the software.

The oldest part of our brain is nicknamed the crocodile brain, which developed as we evolved out of the sea; it is the reptilian brain that is the seat of our unconscious, says Cozolini[9] in his book *The Neuroscience of Psychotherapy*. It's still there, of course, and for good reason. Take, for example, a war situation where your survival may depend on you being able to make a split-second decision. The crocodile brain is good at these split-second decisions, whereas the more evolved rational brain might just be too slow, putting your survival at risk.

As we continued to evolve from reptiles to mammals, the next upgrade was our mammalian brain – the limbic system that is the nurturing, caring part of us. As mammals we care for our young, unlike the crocodile who leaves the eggs to hatch and the young to fend for themselves.

Lastly as we stepped from mammals to Homo sapiens, we developed our neo-cortex, our rational thinking part.

---

[9] Dr Louis Cozolini, *The Neuroscience of Psychotherapy*.

The part that we like to think of as 'us', the smart, logical, rational person we operate as every day, all day!

Unfortunately that is not the case; we still use all of our brain hardware and software. Each of the programs are still running but our crocodile brain is often the loudest and most dominant of the lot because it deals with **3S** stuff – **survival, safety and security, our first key to improved relationships**. We will come to this more fully later in this chapter, because it is absolutely fundamental to understanding our relationships and ourselves. Unbeknown to us our crocodile brain takes over in our day-to-day lives, and quite often to our detriment. Amazing and seemingly ridiculous as this sounds it is the truth. Our crocodiles largely run our show. Consequently it is important that we learn to recognise our own individual crocodile, as its decisions will often impact our lives negatively. Rather than give you a business example here, let's look at a simple husband and wife example because it is more emotive and shows their crocodile brains more clearly. It would be unusual to have this type of overt interaction in the business arena because we usually try and keep better control at work.

A fight

Imagine you and your wife are having an argument about putting out the garbage and it is getting quite heated. Suddenly you are not just shouting about garbage but a whole lot of other things are coming into play, not paying the credit card bill, forgetting her birthday, not noticing that she has changed her hair colour, and on it goes.

How did this escalate? What just happened? Your wife's crocodile brain came into play, she had been feeling unsupported for some time and her crocodile was threatened, her security felt undermined and she was determined things had to change or she was out of the relationship. It was a fight or flight crocodile moment for her. Now you were only vaguely aware that things were starting to go off track so when the fight started you were surprised and startled. Your crocodile went straight into attack and suddenly the situation had escalated dramatically. Your wife was talking of ending the marriage and your crocodile, reacting out of fear, continued to try and shout her down. This prompted her crocodile to fight harder as well. We have all been in similar situations and reacted irrationally. That's our crocodile with no sense of rationality ruling the day and escalating the conflict.

At a conscious, logical level, of course an argument about garbage is not going to threaten your security but on a very different level in your brain, your safety and security may indeed feel vulnerable. After all, this may be the umpteenth time she has complained about how she has to

36

nag you to take out the garbage and it may be the last straw in your relationship. She decides she has had enough and wants to end the marriage. Suddenly it's a very different story. Your safety may not be directly threatened, unless she is so angry she picks up the knife she is cutting vegetables with and lashes out at you, but your security is. Suddenly the assets are going to be split and where you might have felt a comfort in knowing that the mortgage was being slowly paid off, now the amount you will make from selling the house gets halved. Your security feels halved. It all happens in a second, somewhere deep in your brain, while you are busy arguing about garbage. Feeling vulnerable your brain has triggered the 'fight or flight mechanism' and before you know it, you are yelling even louder and the situation deteriorates even more. We think we are in control of our lives but our lives are complex and until we realise what is going on at a much deeper level we are often just reacting emotionally to a stimulus.

Hardwired to survive – the 3Ss

As humans, and like every other creature in this universe, we are hardwired to survive. Our brains want us to be safe. Fundamentally our brain will do everything it can to keep us alive. We have all read amazing stories about people who have survived phenomenal odds and we gravitate to those stories, asking ourselves – given the circumstances, could we survive too?

On the other hand, stories about people who take their own lives somehow sadden us. The majority of us work extremely hard to preserve our life for as long as possible. Modern medicine is an example of how much our society values 'survival' and not necessarily with a good quality of life.

Let's look at the 3Ss from an animal's point of view.

Take our crocodile. A crocodile doesn't question whether to 'Survive' or not; he is hardwired to survive in any way he can. To survive he needs food to get strong. Survival isn't the only thing the crocodile needs to do. He needs to be 'Safe' too. He needs to be strong and fierce enough to fend off bigger crocodiles and find a territory. He needs to hunt, rest and breed, in order to pass on his genes.

If we look at this second S, safety, in human terms we have food so we are surviving – the first S is being fulfilled. But we need to find shelter so we are safe from the elements. This is the second S. Shelter will help prevent us being attacked by others, at least we can barricade the door.

Back to the crocodile and the last of 3Ss, 'Security.' The crocodile will feel much more secure when he is the biggest crocodile around, can mate with all the available females and fight off the other crocodiles who want his patch. When all his 3Ss are satisfied he is one happy crocodile.

Back to us, we have food and water so we can survive. We have a house so we have some safety but now we seek security. We need our job so we can buy our food, pay our mortgage or our rent and be even more secure knowing we have our superannuation. Like the crocodile if we know our larder is full, that we have our house and our job is secure, we can feel we are on the ladder of success.

Status and the 3Ss

The next step is to ensure that our status, which reflects our 3Ss, is on view. This might mean a good car, living in the right suburb, going to restaurants, theatres, operas, concerts, having the designer clothes, fancy jewellery, going to fabulous resorts for our holidays or sending our children to the best schools. These are all signs of status. Our whole industrial world is geared to providing consumers with some level of status, whether it is the smart watch, the great car or having the latest technological gadget.

All sounds simple and obvious but the 3Ss are essentially fundamental feelings that keep us alive and happy. If at any point we unconsciously feel our survival, our safety or our security is being threatened or endangered we will, and do, react. When one of these 3Ss feels shaky it impacts on our relationships, which can start to go horribly wrong.

3Ss in the business context

Let's look what happens to our 3Ss in a business context.

Your boss has asked you to implement an aspect of a plan that you have come up with and he has approved. You started the implementation and he stopped you and got angry that you proceeded. You feel confused, frustrated and angry. After all he had given his approval for the plan; it wasn't as if you were proceeding without permission. You are pleased with your self-control. You didn't explode as you would have liked to do but your boss certainly knew you were angry and cold. As you calm down later you feel uncertain. What is going on? At a deeper level you feel unsure about your job, perhaps he didn't like the plan. Perhaps he was just playing for time; after all the company has been retrenching staff. You feel upset, demotivated and uncertain. Your job security feels threatened.

It is important to understand that unless our 3Ss are satisfied we can't move forward to the next step of our own personal evolution, which is to become the very best of who we are, to realise our full potential. These 3Ss are the pillars that support our higher operating levels.

3 main levels in the brain

Another way to think about all this is to understand that there are three main levels of functioning in the brain:

- The conscious mind – our neo-cortex

- The subconscious

- The unconscious – our crocodile brain

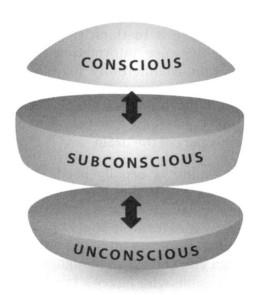

The Conscious Mind

This is the newest part of our brain; it evolved after the unconscious and the limbic system. (That is after we evolved from being crocodiles and mammals and into people.)

We all know that the conscious mind is the part that we think with. It is the newest part of our brain, or the most recently evolved, and is called the neo-cortex. The neo-cortex is thought to be more developed in humans than in any other species on the planet. It is the part that thinks, feels, and acts in the present, in the now. It understands time. The conscious mind evaluates, judges, and observes, it looks and sees. This part of our brain perceives and analyses what is going on and makes decisions based on observations and experiences. We use it to think things through, plan, anticipate, and organise information and ideas. This part of our brain is inherently logical, and wants a rational explanation for everything. The conscious mind is orderly and likes to analyse the cause and effect of ideas, thoughts and actions. The power of criticism also comes from this part of the brain.

The conscious mind is usually used as the gauge in intelligence tests, and is the part of the brain that we generally identify with as who we are. Our lives tend to be dominated by it as it rarely shuts up. If you pause for a moment and concentrate on being present, right here in the now, can you shut your thoughts down for a few seconds? For people who haven't tried meditation this is often a really difficult exercise. The power of the conscious mind is so strong that it wants us continually to be thinking some thought.

So a quick recap on the conscious mind or neo-cortex:

- Newest part of the brain
- Understands time
- Evaluates, judges, observes
- Looks, sees and processes
- Perceives, analyses and makes decisions
- Plans, anticipates and organises information and ideas

- Essentially logical

- Has the power of criticism

- Is usually the gauge in intelligence tests

- Is the part of the brain we identify with and feel is us

Subconscious

There is a difference between the unconscious and the subconscious. Nowadays the words are used interchangeably, but there are three different levels of consciousness: the conscious, the subconscious and the unconscious. For the purposes of this book, I am going to refer to the unconscious as being at a deeper level than the subconscious.

The Oxford dictionary definition of the subconscious is: 'being present in consciousness, and capable of being the subject of, or involving, mental activity, but not fully perceived and recognised by the mind, or completely and clearly present to the attention'.

Sounds confusing? Think of it this way – you are walking down the street, past a bookshop, going about your business, and that night you happen to dream of the bookshop and of a particular book in the window. The next day going past the bookshop, you see that the book that you had dreamt of is in the window. You are surprised because the previous day you were not consciously aware of even looking at the window as you passed, yet your subconscious had absorbed that information. The subconscious is not the same powerhouse as the unconscious. You could think of it as the link that goes between consciousness and the unconscious.

The Unconscious

Now we are really getting to the juicy stuff!

The unconscious is the oldest part of the brain. Part of it is made up of the basal ganglia, and it is the unconscious that we are really going to focus on because it plays havoc with our relationships, without us even realising. Sneaky!

First a quick overview: the unconscious is a collection of modules that operates out of our awareness while we are busy doing other things. For instance our unconscious enables us to breathe without thinking while simultaneously eating and talking. Our unconscious enables us to function efficiently – it is very smart. Your unconscious will make the split-second judgement if you are about to do something dangerous, like step in front of a car while daydreaming as you walk down the street. It will enable you to recall the name of the high school teacher who was fantastic, but which, until you thought about it, was not in your conscious memory. Likewise when you are reading a book your unconscious is hard at work helping you instantly recognise words and their meaning and yet you realise that when you go to turn the page that while you have read the words, your thoughts were miles away.

Our unconscious is automatically processing so much of what we do. Remember earlier we talked about driving a car, when we first learnt there was so much to think about, now for the majority of us we get into a car and we are "in the zone". Like athletes, musicians, artists and any other profession, when we become unconsciously skilled, as opposed to consciously skilled we can operate at our optimum. We are in the 'flow'.

The defining feature of the unconscious is our ability to operate on automatic pilot. It has five key characteristics. It is:

- Non-conscious

- Fast

- Unintentional

- Uncontrollable

- Effortless

All extremely valuable attributes when used in the appropriate place. We learn so much out of conscious awareness, like when we first learnt to talk as children. We were not aware of our learning, it just went into our memory. One of the most important functions of the unconscious is that it absorbs information that threatens our survival faster and better than our conscious minds.

The unconscious is designed to scan the environment quickly and detect patterns easily. But it does not unlearn them well. It is a fairly rigid, inflexible inference-maker. It develops early and continues to guide behaviour into adulthood, says Professor Timothy Wilson in his book, *Strangers to Ourselves: Discovering the Adaptive Unconscious.*[10]

Instant decisions – often out of our control

Our unconscious makes an instant decision when we first meet someone, friend or foe? Do I warm to them or feel cool and distant? Problem is once the unconscious has made up its mind it is very difficult to change. It seems we are hardwired to fit people into categories and leave them there.

If the unconscious has decided that someone is a threat chances are that you will feel uncomfortable around them; and most of the time we don't stop to question that judgement or consciously try and work out why we don't like them. The big disadvantage is that, being set in its habits, our unconscious is slow to respond to new contradictory information and this is where many of our problems with others arise.

Here's the scary part. Even though we feel very much in control of our thoughts and actions, it is actually the unconscious that is responsible for most of our behaviours. That's a fairly terrifying thought because we don't actually have much idea of what goes on in our unconscious at all.

If I asked you what your unconscious is processing at this very moment I bet you would be surprised. Besides being responsible for virtually every thought and action

---

[10] Professor Timothy Wilson, *Strangers to Ourselves: Discovering the Adaptive Unconscious.*

we have, our unconscious processes about 11 million pieces of information per second. Yes you read that right – 11 million pieces of information per second, of which we can only be consciously aware of about 40. How staggering is that?

To register 40 you would still need to be unbelievably aware, perhaps of your breath, of your shoe holding your foot, the moistness of your lips etc. I can only be aware of about 10 as a maximum before I start losing track. But that is how brilliant our unconscious is. Admittedly about 10 million of those pieces of information processed per second come from our ability to see, so we are processing and analysing what our eyes are recording.

Before you start condemning your unconscious for being a rogue thinker and causing all sorts of drama in your life, remember the brilliance of this design. It's a system which allows you to get on with your chosen task at hand, while in the background it keeps everything going, seamlessly, efficiently and effortlessly, constantly reacting and readjusting to the world around you. That's impressive.

Our unconscious is also registering what we feel about everything: whether it is the person walking past your desk or the tone of voice used by the waitress serving your coffee, to how you are feeling about the garbage argument. Our unconscious registers through our five senses and then stores all the information just like an enormous database. Most of what it absorbs we don't consciously retrieve but, like it or not, most of the time it is running our show.

The unconscious playing a major executive role

It plays a major executive role in our mental lives by collecting, interpreting and evaluating information. It "can set goals in motion, quickly and efficiently," says Wilson. It is our unconscious that sees the snake before we can consciously process what we have seen and has made us leap out of the way.

One of the compromises of our super speedy unconscious is that it has no power to discern what is truth from what isn't; what is logical versus what is irrational. The unconscious moves fast and takes everything at face value, with no power to weigh it up. It assumes everything is fact, and as you can imagine this can get us into serious trouble.

If your unconscious thinks the boss is talking harshly to you the chances are you will feel resentful and fed up. Deep down this is because the more primitive crocodile part of our brain is signalling danger – we could be threatened. In fact most of the time when the boss calls you into his office your brain will be on high alert, even if you are not conscious of it. After all he is the larger crocodile on the block and holds more power, which threatens your sense of safety. In today's terms we are so aware of our status as a key indicator of how safe we feel.

When we are in the executive suite, or C suite, we are feeling safer but if the Chairman calls us in to criticise or question an aspect of our management, our crocodile brain jumps to the fore. It doesn't matter what position in the organisation you hold, if the boss calls us in we are aware that our 3Ss could be threatened. However if you are in the executive suite and your executive assistant comes in to ask you what you need him to do your brain is relaxed and feels powerful. We are so tuned in to our status that any perceived undermining will inevitably cause a physical reaction unless we can control it and talk ourselves down from our heightened awareness.

When we are aware that this is a function of the more primitive part of our brain we can, if we feel a flutter of anxiety, tell ourselves this is just our crocodile out to protect us. We can identify the feeling, which helps us gain a sense of control, reflect and engage our neo-cortex, the conscious, rational part of our minds, to analyse what's really going on with the boss. We might see things from a different perspective – for instance, that she is under huge pressure and probably didn't mean to snap at you. This awareness will help us to change our attitude. Our unconscious does not differentiate between what is the truth and what we think is true, but may not be. The power of criticism and evaluation is very much part of the conscious mind.

Food, sex, fight or flight

In his book, *Getting The Love You Want*, Harville Hendrix[11] describes the unconscious mind well when he says, "The only thing your old brain seems to care about is whether a particular person is someone to: 1) nurture, 2) be nurtured by, 3) have sex with, 4) run away from, 5) submit to, or 6) attack. Subtleties such as,

---

[11] Dr Harville Hendrix, *Getting the Love You Want*.

"this is my neighbour," "my cousin," "my mother," or "my wife" slide right on by." In many ways our unconscious mind is very primitive, hence the nickname, crocodile brain.

Eastern philosophy has long used the metaphor of the unconscious as the elephant and the rider as our conscious will. The rider is trying to control the elephant, which doesn't want to be controlled. When you think that the pre-frontal cortex or neo-cortex takes up just 4% of the volume of our brain we can see that the unconscious is a vastly bigger and stronger part of our brain, says David Rock in his book, *Your Brain at Work.*[12]

The unconscious is the seat of our memories, our experiences and everything we have learned. Think of it as similar to your computer – storing everything we have done but incapable of evaluating the validity of the information stored within it. The unconscious's greatest flaw is that it lacks this vital power of criticism and evaluation.

Wilson tells us that the unconscious may be more sensitive to negative information than the conscious self, which can have a huge impact on our fundamental beliefs about ourselves. Most of us grab onto the negative stuff people might say about us and allow the positive to roll straight over our heads. This is because the negative is triggering our 3Ss and as we progress through the 7 keys to empowerment I will talk more about this.

---

[12] Dr David Rock, *Your Brain at Work.*

If you are told often enough that you are stupid then deep down you will believe you are incompetent and it will take a lot of conscious reprogramming to erase that belief. A teacher may tell you that you are hopeless at math and forever after you think you are hopeless at math, until you logically think this through and decide that you can do math; after all, you do it every time you look at your bank balance.

Imagine as a child you have a fearful mother who is often telling you to be careful. Be careful, you could fall, be careful, what you are doing is dangerous, be careful not to talk to strangers they could be dangerous, be careful of cars, you might get run over, be careful of power points, the electricity could kill you, be careful of water, you might drown. All of these are typical things we may tell a toddler umpteen times over a number of years in order to keep him safe, and if his Mum is always modelling the same fearful behaviour this is what he will learn. It drops into his unconscious and then it is hardly surprising that the toddler turns into a fearful adult who has an unconscious belief that the world is not safe.

As an employee it's possible that he will turn out to be very much a 'yes' man, less confident in his own opinion because it could be wrong. This restricts his imagination and creativity, so he is not bringing all of who he is and all of his abilities into the work arena. Remember what we said about systems? This employee would probably be the person who at an unconscious level believes that you, as boss, should look after him like his Mum always did.

Our unconscious – often the root cause of relational problems

An important concept to grasp is that once the unconscious mind has been programmed in a certain way that will, rightly or wrongly, become our truth. And even when we realise the belief is not serving us it takes considerable awareness to break the habit.

And this is why so many of our relationships can go wrong without us knowing why or how. Often we are operating on 'truths' that were laid down when we were children, growing, learning and reacting to the environment around us. Sometimes those 'truths' and that programming are outdated and irrelevant to our present-day situations, yet we still base our behaviour on them.

We have now learnt a lot about our brain and you may be thinking this is interesting stuff but how is it relevant? **It is relevant because our brain, particularly our unconscious, is usually the root cause of problems in relationships.**

As a business leader it is right here, at this fundamental level, that issues start. In the work environment we have to appear to be in control, capable and sophisticated. We wouldn't get a job if we were really in contact with this fundamental element of our personality and allowed it to be clearly seen. The scary thing is that most of us are totally unaware that the crocodile part of our brain is motivating our behaviour and causing the problems that all of us encounter in life, or at work at one time or another. The disguise to appear to be in control is a very carefully constructed persona that we all create. We create it so well that it appears to be, not a disguise, but who we are – and what's more we believe it is who we are. When we become more conscious of the power of our crocodile brain we would be able to be more of the rational person we like to think we are.

7 Keys

Below once again are the seven keys to facilitate and enable successful relationships and enhance both your career and personal life. You have already covered the first key point in this chapter. Don't worry if you don't quite understand the rest of them now because you will as you read on.

1. All our behaviour is initially motivated by 3s: **Survival, Safety and Security** (crocodile brain). (This first key to relationship success we have already explored and it provides the foundation of the other six points.)

2. Our instinctive drive to protect ourselves often causes emotional reactivity and destructive patterns in our relationships.

3. Our thinking patterns and behaviour today remain largely untouched since programming was laid down in early childhood.

4. This programming went into the unconscious and we do not realise that our unconscious influences our every thought and action.

5. (Do you remember learning to drive? There was a lot to master, but now driving is second nature, you don't even think about it, you just do it. Our behaviour, attitude and thinking is also like this, embedded into our unconscious).

6. Our programming taught us to hide what was not considered acceptable behaviour and it sank into our unconscious (cognitive dissonance).

7. To avoid looking at our own less than perfect characteristics we focus on others' faults – PROJECTION.

Our projections influence the way we think about others, and that in turn affects our behaviour.

Chapter Recap

There are three wonderfully complex layers within our brain - the conscious, the subconscious and the unconscious.

All our behaviour is directly motivated by the 3Ss – survival, safety and security.

This comes from our unconscious, whose main purpose is to ensure our survival and keep us safe. When the 3Ss are in place we seek to improve our status.

Our conscious is the rational thinking part that is essentially logical. We identify with this part of ourselves the most.

Our unconscious brain (or crocodile brain) is primal and an exceptionally effective system, which operates outside of our awareness enabling fast and adaptive mental processing of billions of bytes of information.

The unconscious has no evaluative powers so it perceives situations as the whole truth when in reality it may not be the truth at all.

This process can be incredibly destructive to our relationships.

Your journey

Can you identify incidents at work when, with the benefit of reflection, you realise that your crocodile brain was reactive?

Can you recall incidents at work when you exercised strong self-control? That was your neo-cortex working.

Can you think of people in your life that you would like to **imagine** your crocodile attacking? If so, now you know you are truly human! Can you now imagine your neo-cortex coming into play to control that urge and initiate peace?

Chapter 3

The second key: our instinctive drive to protect ourselves often causes emotional reactivity and destructive patterns of interpersonal interaction

Building on what we've learnt in the previous chapter about the 3Ss, our conscious mind and our crocodile brain, we now know that our unconscious instinctively interprets situations at lightning speed.

What we will cover in more detail in this chapter is that our parents and caregivers programmed our unconscious as we grew. For the moment it is important to understand that our parents continually modelled all the rules and ways to behave, which dropped into our unconscious to effectively become our blueprint or hard drive. This programming from early childhood has a direct influence on how we think and behave in our relationships. The next important fact to know is that how we think about something directly influences how we view a situation, whether it is positive or negative.

Let's jump back briefly to the neuroscience. To be efficient we know that our crocodile brain doesn't like to change its mind once it has accepted and programmed in something as a truth. We also like to be right at least 90% of the time and we are clever at selecting only the information and evidence that supports our view, while ignoring facts that point in a different direction.

The science of social psychology teaches us that we will see only what we want to see. Like a physical immune system, our psychological immune system works to keep the world the way we want to see it, says Prof Wilson.

The ramifications of this are far-flung because we want to convince others that our opinion is the right one and often the only correct one! How often have you tried to convince others that you are right? Certainly I know I want to be right much of the time!

If we are in a work situation we might try and persuade others into feeling what we are feeling, which can lead to the formation of negative cliques. We are unconsciously primed to notice what we may perceive as a conspiratorial group talking away. You are pretty sure they are not talking about business and wonder what they are talking about. Your 3Ss are aroused whether you are aware of your brain's inner activities or not.

Or, on a personal front, when we disagree with a spouse or sibling how often do we go off and try and enlist our friends' support against the 'bad' other. This tactic is called **triangulation.**

We are not being deliberately manipulative when we try to bring others in to support our view, we do it unconsciously to try and build support and solidarity for ourselves. (Again the 3Ss come into play.) Most of us don't enjoy being out on a limb; we want to pull others in to side with us. This particularly evident in a business environment where you will often hear the gossip over the coffee machine as we try and pull our work colleagues into sharing our particular gripe about someone.

Coming back to wanting to be right, the scary thing is that the more often we think something and convince ourselves it is right, the more truth that thought holds for us and it literally shapes our physical brain connections.

"Where you focus your attention, you make connections", says neuroscientist Jeffrey Schwartz.[13] Focus your attention on something new, and you make new connections. This has been shown to be true through studies of neuroplasticity, where focused attention plays a critical role in creating physical changes in the brain.

You could think of it as water running down the easiest path. Gradually it wears away a bigger and bigger track. The same with our brain – the more we think a particular thought the more entrenched the neural pathways become in our brain. The more I think I dislike a particular person or situation, the more difficult it becomes to change that way of thinking. It has started to carve a deep pathway in my brain.

The need to be right

One of our major internal battles rages between our need to be accurate and our desire to feel good about ourself. How we wage this battle and how it is won are the central determinants of who we are and how we feel

---

[13] Jeffrey Schwartz, in conversation with Dr David Rock.

about ourselves, says Wilson. There are major ramifications for us, not only in our personal but also in our business relationships, when we continually think we are right and that the other is lacking. We need to be aware of this very human predisposition because it leads to irrational assumptions.

There is a lovely story (probably totally untrue) that clearly illustrates this point:

A battleship and what appears to be another vessel are on a collision course and the captain of the battleship requests the other vessel to change course. The other vessel responds that the battleship should change course and an argument ensues with the captain of the battleship becoming more heated and talking of his superior size. Eventually the other 'vessel' says it's your call, I'm a lighthouse!

We can clearly see the battleship captain's crocodile brain at play. He did not want to change his mind and was counting on his superior size! We all fall into this trap at one time or another – it starts in kindergarten. For a while we can blame it on our crocodile brain that wants to be right to feel safe and secure, but after we become aware this won't work if we want to evolve.

We want to make our own decisions and carry out those decisions, or be given the autonomy to do what we want to do; because of course we feel we know best. When we have the authority our crocodile brain feels in control and safer. However often when we are given autonomy we want the support of others to back us up. This has the added benefit of covering our back and being able to blame others if it all goes wrong. In the business environment we all want autonomy because it gives us a sense of self-importance, status and control. We want to build our own empire.

Another aspect to consider in our desire to be right is the difficulty most of us have in truly hearing another person without our own subjectivity, emotional and feeling responses getting in the way. Most of the time we don't listen carefully to what another is saying. We sort of assume we know and then are anxious to put our own point of view forward, often not having truly heard what the other person wanted to communicate.

If we focus hard on what the other is saying we can start to hear all the underlying messages. Addressing these or at least being curious about them takes the focus away from our self and makes our communications flow much more easily. This desire to be right is particularly prevalent at work, largely because we are generally more alert to possible criticism. Our third S, security, could be threatened. Hence at work we will often hear justification and excuses.

A useful exercise is to practise listening. Get someone to tell you something about a problem they are having. After listening carefully, paraphrase what you think they said, and ask them if you understood correctly. It's a shock to think we have listened to someone and then they tell us we haven't really heard what they have said, or perhaps what has been implied. This happens more often than you would expect. (Try using this technique with your nearest and dearest, because they will feel properly heard, and you will get them onside!)

Reactive Behaviour

When someone disagrees with us or we misunderstand what he or she is saying because of our own unconscious bias, it's easy to get angry and frustrated. This emotion is linked to the crocodile brain's interpretation that we are being threatened. What happens when we feel threatened? Below are just a few examples of behaviour that we all probably exhibit at some stage or another, or perhaps feel we have experienced at the hands of another.

- Competition (fear others will be perceived as better than me)

- Lack of cooperation

- Aggressiveness

- Deceit – lying, cheating

- Manipulation

- Withdrawal of recognition and/or lack of recognition

- Frustration at not being fully heard

- Perceived favouritism

- Territorial/empire building as a power base

- Failure to understand the part we play

These are known as positioning strategies, intended – maybe not consciously – to try and get the upper hand. We believe if we get the upper hand we will be safe.

Again this is the crocodile brain in action. (We are seeking to resolve the threat and therefore feel safe.) If we stop, engage our neo-cortex and think things through, we might see that, while some of these behaviours and strategies may give us a short-term advantage, it will not be in our long-term interest. Remember, crocodiles probably don't think about their long-term future – it is about survival and dominance now.

Jane was concerned that her co-worker Melinda was getting more positive attention from the boss than she felt she deserved. Jane decided it was because Melinda was young and attractive, so she set out to undermine her in any way she could. The company's structure was that new sales information came across Jane's desk first. This made it easy for her to withhold information and try to make Melinda look as if she was out of touch with the latest developments. Eventually Melinda became dispirited with feeling undermined and left. In the short term Jane had appeared to win.

Surprising though it may seem, we learnt all of these positioning strategy behaviours in childhood. We may not have been subtle or sophisticated in how we implemented them but if you think of the playground I have no doubt you would recognise each and every strategy – each one motivated by our 3Ss.

Often it seems that the same thing is happening in our business environment except now we are dressed in suits rather than shorts and shirts or dresses. And we work hard to disguise what we are doing, while it is easy to see the behaviour in small children. Almost without fail these tactics lead to a lack of personal satisfaction in the longer term.

Arguably, the worst thing about this is that our crocodile brain doesn't take any responsibility for our part in fiery interactions. Crocodiles don't like saying sorry; the word doesn't feature in their vocabulary. And remember our unconscious believes that its perspective is 'truth' and therefore it is always someone else's fault. However the other people involved in the situation, are also at the whim of their crocodile brains and are likely to be acting in a similar way, particularly if they feel threatened.

So here we have a picture of two crocodiles facing each other off. Not a pretty sight, and if one of the crocodiles is more powerful than the other, he/she will generally win the fight and the less powerful one will withdraw, perhaps to fight again later, or try and engage in some strategy to outwit the bigger crocodile.

Deceit, manipulation, undermining, resentment and sabotage all spring to mind as ways to counteract the bigger crocodile. In the business arena going on a go-slow or on strike would be a typical example of getting revenge on the powers that be ... in the short term.

Chapter Recap

Once our crocodile brain has made up its mind, it doesn't like changing it.

Our crocodile brain only really wants to see and hear what it wants to see and hear (lighthouse story.)

Neither of which may be fact, or even reasonably accurate!

Crocodile brain wants to be right and it wants the autonomy to do what it wants to do.

We will try and convince others that our opinions are correct in order to shore up a base of support. This forms little cliques. We may do this unconsciously.

When we feel threatened we can become very reactive in our behaviour including aggression, deceit, sabotage and manipulation.

We don't want to take any responsibility for the part we play in the interaction; it is usually someone else's fault.

The other people involved in the fiery interaction or relationship are also at the mercy of their crocodile brain and may be reacting and behaving in the same way you are.

Your journey

Can you think of incidents at work when you have felt convinced your proposed course of action was appropriate and should have been the one adopted? With the benefit of reflection now, was that the case? Could the other person have been proposing a valid alternative?

Can you think of occasions when you have been so convinced that you are correct that you did not want to listen to another's perspective?

Can you think of incidents when someone did not want to listen to you? How did it make you feel and did it impact your ongoing relationship?

Chapter 4

The third key: our thinking patterns and behaviour today remain largely untouched and unnoticed since programming was laid down in early childhood

Your brain is like the hardware of an incredibly powerful computer, but you've been operating on software programming that was installed when you were a toddler! Is it time for an upgrade?

This is a scary thought. Most of us are totally unaware that we work today on understandings and experiences that we absorbed in the first few years of our life. Imagine driving a car today that is 20, 30 or 40 years old. No power steering or power-assisted brakes, no radio, no electric windows, no heating or air conditioning, and the list goes on. Well, psychologically that is what many of us are doing today – running on value systems laid down into our unconscious by our well-meaning parents or caregivers.

Many of us are working from belief systems that may not even be our own. We are on autopilot reacting from ideas laid down in our unconscious, often before we had even developed any rational powers of critical evaluation.

In all fairness to our parents and caregivers they were doing the best job they could and they needed to socialise the little crocodile within us, as we, in turn, socialise the little crocodiles we bring into the world. As babies we yelled when we were hungry, wet, or cold and wanted instant attention. Our brain in those very early months of development was just like a little crocodile's. We had to survive and our survival instinct was very strong. Gradually we developed and grew, our limbic system kicked in, and we realised other people had different preferences to us. We often see 2-4 year olds and older children looking at the new baby in the family and bringing him or her a bottle or a toy. This is the nurturing limbic system in play.

The last part of our brain to switch on was our thinking rational part. Generally speaking the neo-cortex is slowly coming on line at ages 3 to 4. We've all seen toddler tantrums. This is because the neo-cortex isn't available and therefore very small children do not have the skill of reason, much to our frustration as adults.

Truth – or not?

At this age, when our little brains have so much to absorb, everything our parents and our environments tell us gets perceived as truth – Father Christmas, magic and monsters are perceived to be real. Our parents had the unenviable task of trying to socialise us and turn us into civilised little people that didn't run amuck, taking others' toys, bullying and generally being totally self-absorbed. We were taught the rules of the family and the society we grew up in so that the family could function effectively and efficiently. All this programming was encoded into our unconscious when we had no evaluative powers to decide its value. Our parental programming formed the blueprint of our lives.

We are generally unaware that this programming is there and underlying all our initial gut reactions. Its power and influence on our everyday actions is enormous.

Are you asking what relevance does this all this information about our wonderfully powerful computer brain and early programming have on my business? Another good question!

Great leaders understand what is going on under the competent façade people initially present when we are deciding they would fit in well with our team and help us build profitability. The more we understand about this fundamental programming the more equipped we will be, not only to know ourselves, but to make more informed choices.

Neuroscience and Emotions

So let's dive into the neuroscience again.

We know that the brain is genetically programmed and develops and matures as a result of ongoing experience. Experience shapes the brain throughout life by altering the neuron connections within the brain. We have literally trillions of neuron connectors and each time we do something new we build more connectors. All mental processes are created by the activity of neurons firing in the brain. Each experience we have gives rise to an emotional response or reaction. Remember the first time you saw the sea or played in snow, went ice skating or dancing. Perhaps your first kiss or sexual experience. Each of these sensual experiences generated an emotional response, which perhaps you don't remember but which is nevertheless recorded in your personal database, your unconscious. Their influences will in all probability still be playing out today. You may love or hate the sea, the snow, or dancing and that emotional response will largely stem from those very first experiences, depending on whether they were good or bad. If they were good you probably love the experience.

The emotions we feel in connection with experiences, people and situations are a fundamental integrating process within the brain and influence our social response.

You are at the disco with your friend because she loves to dance. But you hate it; the loud music really puts you off, as do all the people crowded together on a small dance floor, throwing themselves around. You can't think of anything worse and you don't know why you feel as strongly as you do. What your conscious mind doesn't remember, but your unconscious does, is that way back in your past as a toddler you were exposed to a very noisy big family party at Christmas where there was lots of loud music and big people dancing around. You felt lost in the crowd amongst all the legs and couldn't find your parents. It was a frightening experience for you. That fearful feeling has imprinted itself in your memory and was stored in your unconscious. While you didn't remember the circumstances well it has strongly impacted your current opinion about discos, loud music and feeling trapped in a small space with lots of moving bodies.

> *Another example: As a small boy you experienced the absolute horror the day Dad came home and said he had lost his job and that there would be no more money coming in. Everything was going to change and the house may have to be sold because he would not be able to pay the mortgage. Engraved on your memory at that moment would be the thought that the workplace could be unpredictable and life could change instantly. That response has embedded itself deep into your psyche and whenever there is any office talk of retrenchments you feel your stress level rise dramatically.*

Experiences shape our worldview

Our experiences influence how we view the world. Each experience generates its own perspective or state of mind that directly impacts our picture of the world and how we respond to each and every circumstance. If most of our early experiences were positive and we trusted our parents to take good care of us, we will have probably formed an optimistic view of the world and live life accordingly. If however you were bought up in a war zone and life was dangerous and unpredictable, you would probably have a fearful, untrusting view of the world.

Emotion and social connection go hand-in-hand. When people feel our emotion, such as feeling happy or sad for us, or we share an emotion, we feel connected, seen or heard. When we feel seen we feel good and our feelings have been given resonance and reflection. Of course the reverse also applies. When we feel unheard, disconnected or alone in our feelings, we feel dissatisfied or sad. These feelings of emotional connection or disconnection are called **emotional resonance**. What happens in relationships stems from emotional resonance, either positive or negative. It underlies relationships. For example when we feel slight discomfort in an interaction we instinctively know and feel the emotional resonance is off key.

If it is not quite right we may not be able to put a finger on exactly why. It is quite likely that the other person is not feeling at ease either and it may be all about them, but you are picking up the energy and that's emotional resonance. Socially it feels uncomfortable. When both parties feel happy and connected emotional resonance feels right. Again in the business environment you know immediately what sort of mood your boss is in when you go to ask him something. You have read either his emotional openness or his closed mindset and you quickly re-evaluate whether you will go ahead with your request or quietly withdraw to await a more conducive atmosphere.

Let's jump back to the neuroscience again. Although we have a crocodile brain we also have a limbic system (the caring part) and a neo-cortex (rational, thinking) both newer parts of our brains, which are profoundly relational. We could not survive as a species without being supported by each other. We couldn't live as babies and children without being looked after, so our brains have evolved to be profoundly relational.

Fairness

As humans we are particularly geared to recognising fairness. Remember as children how we would be so aware of what was fair and what wasn't. When your brother or sister got something you didn't you would be the first to notice and complain. Again this is the older parts of our brain, both crocodile and mammal, coming into play. Our brain evolved to be able to spot who to trust and who was less trustworthy.

This came from being hunter-gatherers. If we killed the bison we couldn't eat it all, with no refrigeration, so would share it out amongst our tribe. This instigated a type of trust system. We had to trust that the person we had given some of our bison to would return the favour when he killed the next bison. If we found that we didn't receive our fair share we would know not to trust that person next time. We learnt the hard way how to identify friend, foe or those who were purely indifferent to our needs. We are good at reading all the signs and fairness is a large signpost for us. Our brain is always checking for fairness particularly in our working environment where we are all supposed to be treated fairly. The rise of unionism, with its power of numbers, was one way of ensuring fairness.

We have survived and flourished as a species because we can respond readily and accurately to another's intentions. One of the ways the brain does this is by using mirror neurons.

Mirror neurons

Mirror neurons serve to link the emotional expression of one person to another. For example, when we see another person cry we may feel like crying or even cry, although not so likely in a business environment. Likewise if we see someone angry we may also feel angry. This is why a good movie can be such an emotional roller coaster ride. Our mirror neurons detect or read another's intention. Mirror neurons, as well as a creative imagination, also may help us to feel how another is feeling and enables us to put ourselves in their shoes, by checking how our own body/mind responds. This is the basis of empathy and compassion. We can instinctively read a situation and can gauge friend or foe.

One implication of this skill is that as small children we will have instinctively gauged our parents' reaction to different situations and this will have dropped down into our unconscious to influence, unbeknown to us, our perceptions of the world.

Being aware of this enables us to quietly question our beliefs to ensure that we are acting out of our own belief systems and not just parroting old beliefs that may no longer serve us, or being walking facsimiles of our parents. Reprogramming ourselves, takes constant repetition in order to create new neural pathways to undo our early encoding. Every time a situation occurs our brain immediately searches our memory banks for a similar experience and the outcome of that initial situation will largely determine our reactions to the current situation. So, without us being aware we are continually dragged back to old pathways usually from many years before. "Issues from our past may influence us in the present and alter how we behave in the future by directly shaping how we perceive what is going on around us and inside us," says Siegel.[14]

Before closing this chapter about how our brain has been encoded let's briefly look at what two experts have to say.

Daniel Kahneman,[15] a Nobel Prize winner for his revolutionary work in psychology, talks about the unconscious bias we all have. He describes our two ways of thinking as System 1 and System 2.

System 1 is the fast, automatic, easy thinking that comes from the unconscious and System 2 is much slower and more considered coming from the neo-cortex. (System 1 thinking overlaps with our fast, crocodile thinking.) Kahneman goes on to say System 1 is automatically biased and is not necessarily logical. It is based on our beliefs and we then find reasons to justify our beliefs. "We think that we have reasons but in fact we first have the belief and then we accept the reasons," says Kahneman.

This has obvious ramifications for managing people. We will make some fundamental mistakes if we assume that everyone shares a similar belief system even if we are culturally aligned. Our beliefs are the product of our childhood environment and often do not change unless

---

[14] Dr Daniel Siegel, *The Developing Mind.*
[15] Dr Daniel Kahneman, talking to Nigel Warburton from Social Science Bites.

we consciously look at them and decide if they still serve us and correspond with our current thinking. Our predisposition will be to assume our beliefs are the correct ones and our crocodile brain will find all the reasons to support those beliefs.

SCARF model

David Rock talking about his SCARF model[16] describes some key aspects that he thinks are vital for good management to recognise and heed, which stem directly from the way our brain works. Rock talks about Status, Certainty, Autonomy, Relatedness and Fairness. If we can understand our own need for these to be met in our life we are well ahead of the game when it comes to understanding and managing others.

Status – we are continually aware of our status because it relates directly to our crocodile brain. To feel safe our brain wants us to be the top crocodile so any perceived erosion of status, including the smallest of put-downs, is interpreted as our 3Ss being undermined or threatened. Our crocodile comes to the fore in plotting how to regain status, whether it is by undermining the person who has the status or ingratiating ourselves to the person with the higher status, so we benefit. This is disruptive to productivity in the work environment. The perceived undermining of status can be as small as turning to one person in the meeting for a comment and not to another. The one not included is more than likely to react in some way, usually negatively.

---

[16] Dr David Rock, *Our Brain at Work.*

Certainty – we all unconsciously crave certainty so that we feel safe. We go to endless lengths to control in order to feel a certainty in our world but as we have learnt from the theory of complexity there is no such thing as unchanging certainty. To evolve we continually need to change. In our desire for certainty we want transparency and openness because then we can get a sense of how things are going to pan out and therefore be prepared. This need for certainty, transparency and openness has important implications for management.

Autonomy – again in an attempt to secure certainty we want autonomy to give us a sense of control as well as importance. We all feel we are right at least 90% of the time and autonomy proves it to ourselves.

Relatedness – we have seen how our brains have evolved to be profoundly relational; we could not have survived as a species if this wasn't the case.

Fairness – we know that again our brains are extremely quick to notice fairness and will react negatively if we perceive unfairness.

All of these aspects come from both our crocodile and mammalian brains and we need to use our neo-cortex to become aware and react from a conscious rather than an unconscious level.

Chapter Recap

The blueprint of our lives comes from our parental programming.

This blueprint was encoded when we were extremely young (1-5 years) and before our conscious thinking, evaluative neo-cortex was developed.

Most of us are still operating on that same programming today and are often unaware of it.

Our experiences directly influence how we look at the world and how we respond now and in the future.

Emotion and social connections form a linking process with experience to shape our view of reality, our beliefs, attitudes and behaviour. We are particularly attuned to fairness and trust.

The emotions we feel dictate how we view the world and direct how we engage with the world around us.

Key elements for managers to recognise as vital are people's unconscious bias, their need for status, certainty, autonomy, relatedness and fairness (SCARF).

Your journey

Are there incidents in your life when you have decided that you no longer wanted to think a particular way? You recognised that your old thinking no longer served you or was no longer applicable

Can you think of occasions in the office when, with additional information, you changed your mind and your perception of someone or something?

How have experiences that you considered unfair impacted you?

In your business life have you felt your status has been compromised in some way, and how that made you feel?

Chapter 5

The fourth key: programming went into the unconscious and we do not realise that our unconscious influences our every thought and action

What we have learnt so far is that our programming and much of our belief system was formed out of conscious awareness and has been set deep into our unconscious mind. Even more frightening is the influence that programming is having on our every thought and action.

We were taught the rules of our family at a very young age, often in very subtle ways. Misbehaviour could be noted with the mere raising of an eyebrow, a look or a feeling of being dismissed, not seen, and ignored. Often the messages were the same as our own parents had received as children and passed on with no conscious awareness.

The following example shows how subtle this can all be: you knew you had stepped out of line when Dad raised his eyebrow at you as a child. Raised eyebrows become a trigger for you; they signal danger to our crocodile brain. Perhaps today your boss raises her eyebrows when she feels your work is inadequate in some way. That gesture immediately sends a signal to your brain – be aware, danger is around the corner. You may feel infuriated towards her without knowing why.

Usually our immediate reaction to feeling uncomfortable is to find fault with the other, either overtly or covertly. In this case we may feel real resentment towards the boss, which then plays out in some way. You could try and pull your co-workers into feeling the same way you do about the boss or you could try and sabotage the boss in some way, undermine her or merely make the atmosphere really uncomfortable.

Back to our programming: parents in an effort to help as well as control their children also try and instil drivers or motivational rules. A few common ones are:

- Don't
- Please others – think of others
- Do as you are told
- Work hard
- Hurry up
- We know best
- Be perfect

There is a wonderful little 'should' list by famous psychotherapist Virginia Satir who wrote:

"Rules for Being a Good Person
I must always be:
Right
Clean
Bright

Sane
Good
Observant
Healthy
No matter what the cost of the situation
For
Everyone counts more than I
And
Who am I to ask for anything for myself?"

I wonder how many of us resonate with some aspect of the above. Can you still remember the frequent criticisms of yourself that you heard as a child and which may still quietly plague you? We talked earlier about how our unconscious may be more sensitive to negative information than our rational, thinking, neo-cortex, our conscious self. These negative comments usually leave deep scars and often impact on our fundamental beliefs about our self. Negative messages, particularly those received early in life, often act as drivers, which can bring great success in life but sometimes with a high emotional cost. We now know that positive reinforcement is much more productive.

Shaped by others

Our sense of self and our sense of our own identity are defined by our relationships and the way we connect with others, says Siegel.[17] It is shaped both on an emotional and physiological level. Our sense of 'I' is profoundly influenced by how we belong to the group of people around us, the 'we'. We construct the narrative

---

[17] Dr Dan Siegel, *The Developing Mind.*

of our lives based on the social context we live in. For example if people think poorly of us, that is going to have a very detrimental effect on who we think we are and what we believe we are capable of. Conversely if people think highly of us, this is likely to buoy our confidence and our sense of self.

When we are very young our unconscious is particularly attuned to criticism and negativity because it is so vital for us to feel safe and secure. This is why and how our parents and caregivers could exert so much power. That little look or a comment like: 'I will deal with you later' had real influence. It largely taught us obedience; it was safer to obey the rules. Somehow our survival instinct knew that we would be helpless and unlikely to survive if we displeased our parents too much, so we became conditioned.

Not all bad news

Before you try to throw off all the social constructs that your parents plugged into your unconscious, remember that ... these rules and 'shoulds' are not all bad news, says Eric Berne,[18] (who taught us Transactional Analysis or TA as it is commonly known). The unconscious and the rules we have absorbed as children largely govern our life and "liberation from these influences is no easy matter, since they are deeply ingrained and are necessary during the first two or three decades of life for biological and social survival ... children do have some discretion as to which parts of their parents' teachings they will accept ... because the

---

[18] Dr Eric Berne, *Games People Play*.

adaptation was a series of decisions, albeit largely unconscious, they can be undone, since decisions are reversible under favourable circumstances".[19]

Being set up for failure

We can't change what we are unaware of, which is why becoming aware and learning all of this is important and useful. It gives us the opportunity to think about and examine what rules and drivers we have influencing our lives. Even the drivers (those phrases designed to drive us on) such as, work harder, be good and the multitude of others we hear as children – while seeming innocuous and even helpful at the time – could in fact be setting us up for failure, mainly because it's impossible to always fulfil them. We can't always be everything to everybody and work hard and be perfect. We are human and we make mistakes.

When we fail to live up to these pre-programmed drivers and expectations we castigate ourselves, and judge ourselves as failures. Negative self-talk starts and continues its vicious cycle, etching itself ever more deeply into the fabric of our being and physically into our brains. (Self-talk is the mind telling us what to do and think.) It generally keeps up an incessant chatter, which is the only way it knows of fighting to protect us from emotional pain. Unfortunately its thoughts are often obsessive, repetitive and compulsive, which only adds to our discomfort. (Have a listen right now and hear what your self-talk is saying.) Dr Tony Grant,

---

[19] Dr Eric Berne, *Games People Play.*

Associate Professor of the University of Sydney, calls these 'ANTS', Automatic Negative Thoughts.

Continually operating under an injunction like 'try harder' sets us up for continual self-criticism. It is important to remind ourselves that it is far healthier and more encouraging to acknowledge what we have achieved, and to give ourselves and others positive reinforcements, than to dwell on what we and others haven't achieved up to now.

Many of these rules work well for business. If we have absorbed the rule we must work hard it is likely that we will be in the office early and may be one of the last to leave. If we feel that we are not successful enough we will drive ourselves to work even harder in an attempt to feel more successful and more content.

But while the drivers may work well for business they do not necessarily make for a rounded individual who will often be more creative and well-balanced than a workaholic. If the workaholic doesn't get the recognition he or she feels they deserve the resentment sets in and they may resort to some less desirable characteristics. Extraordinary as it may seem to us as responsible adults, today we are still driven by what we didn't get as children.

Unconscious, unmet childhood needs motivate our behaviour

The way we were as children doesn't go away when we grow up. We've looked at how it remains a dynamic part of us through our unconscious programming. What we don't necessarily acknowledge is its power to motivate our current experiences. If we didn't get what we needed as children (and it is worth emphasising that none of us ever had, or could have, the perfect childhood), we continue to seek what we really need through our adult relationships. **Our unmet childhood needs for security and approval continue to haunt all our relationships, until they become conscious.**

We want from our spouses, partners, bosses what we didn't get as children. The aspects of our 3Ss that didn't get met continue to plague us. A man's desire for a secure job with sufficient superannuation may stem directly from seeing his parents struggle financially when he was a child. In his desire to be secure he may stay in a safe but boring position and thereby deny himself the opportunity of trying to be all he could be.

Paul thinks he is always one step ahead of the boss, that he is better and brighter than his boss. This may have come from his childhood of wanting to be good at sports because his Dad loved watching all the sports on television. It seemed the only way to get his Dad's attention was to be as good a sportsman as the people his Dad was watching. However he was more of an academic than a natural sportsman and his Dad wasn't really interested in his puny sporting efforts. As a man Paul married a sporty woman and then was forever trying to keep up with his athletic wife and cope with her frustration that he couldn't keep up with her either running or cycling. As compensation for his frustration and his yearning for recognition he sees himself as better than those around him at work and is not above claiming others' ideas and putting them forward to his boss as his own. Unfortunately for him his attitude has the unfortunate consequence of making him unpopular with his workmates, which just further aggravates his need for recognition, turning it all into a vicious cycle.

....

Sheila craved to be told she was special as she often heard her younger sister being told she was exceptional. She tried so hard to hear the same thing said about her but never did. As an employee Sheila continually wants her boss's approval and keeps trying to ingratiate herself into his favour. As a boss you know this person is wanting more than you are prepared to give, she asks too many personal questions and wants to encourage in chat rather than work. At first her interest is flattering, but it quickly becomes irritating. When you try and give her feedback that you are too busy to be able to spend the time with her she becomes emotional and then resentful, because as she tells you, she is only trying to do her best.

....

The same can apply to a male working for a female boss. At an unconscious level he thinks of her as Mum and tries hard to please. Tim has a female boss whom he feels is far too quick to criticise his work, which makes his blood boil. However Tim's reaction is far more emotive than is logically reasonable. What Tim doesn't realise is that at an unconscious level his boss's criticism reminds him of his somewhat distant, critical, cold mother. If Tim could consciously become aware of this he could exercise some control over his angry reaction and be more open to taking on board his boss's comments.

As a child Jane learnt to be a 'good' girl and being assertive was dangerous behaviour. Consequently as an adult Jane is passive which stops her corporate progression because she is uncomfortable managing a team.

That is how unconscious ideas, decisions and desires, that we had no idea we had, or were making, rule our lives. To a greater or lesser extent they dictate our everyday actions and interactions.

The way to stop this cycle is to become aware and become conscious of these patterns. Self-awareness and understanding can free us from the imprisoning inflexible thoughts laid down in childhood. This is where some personal reflection is needed so that, armed with this personal knowledge, we can understand why we become emotionally reactive.

Chapter Recap

As children we were socialised to fit into the family hierarchy.

We were all taught rules, many of which were unspoken and subtly reinforced.

We obeyed because it kept us safer and more secure (less threatening for our 3Ss.)

These rules were programmed into our unconscious, absorbed as truth and went unquestioned.

This laid down a blueprint for how we should behave, what was acceptable and what was not.

Most of our behaviour today may be still coming from those old injunctions, rules and drivers. For the most part they are out of our conscious awareness.

When we start to self-reflect we can get a handle on those beliefs and their usefulness and decide whether to keep them, or update them.

Unless we become aware, this programming will also underlie all future interactions

Unconscious, unmet childhood needs can still motivate our behaviour at a very profound level.

With self-reflection and conscious awareness of why we react the way we do, we have more choice about how we behave.

Your journey

Spend some time reflecting on what values drive your behaviour.

Are those drivers helpful to you?

Do they make you feel good about yourself? If not are they right for you today?

Can you think of incidents at work where your drivers have had a negative impact on either you or your work colleagues?

What steps will you take to change the drivers that do not work for you?

Chapter 6

The fifth key: our programming taught us to hide what was considered unacceptable behaviour and it sank into our unconscious (cognitive dissonance)

Probably the first question you will ask is what on earth is **cognitive dissonance?**

It is a psychological concept that in the simplest terms means we don't want to know about something if it's too uncomfortable. It is the discomfort we feel when we find ourselves doing things that don't fit with what we know, or having opinions that do not fit with other opinions we hold. For example, we know we should credit the person that came up with the great marketing idea yet we don't want to lose the kudos it has brought. So while we feel uncomfortable stealing someone's idea we do it anyway and feel somewhat awkward.

Another example: we know we should not steal and we try very hard to be honest, but we claim expenses that are not legitimate in our tax return. Was cognitive dissonance at play when the Australian Wheat Board initially denied that they were making illegal payments to the Iraqi government which were labelled transportation fees in breach of UN regulations; or when Leightons, a major Australian construction company, was accused of bribery and corruption in various different countries over the last few years?

We try hard to reduce the discomfort we feel around those decisions.

A personal example that really bought this concept home to me happened when my baby son Max was sitting in the supermarket trolley. As I unloaded the groceries into the car the trolley got lighter, rolled away, and then flipped over. Max fell out and started crying with a bleeding mouth. I felt awful – why didn't I foresee what would happen. I scooped him up and took him home. Later when my husband came home I told him what had happened and he looked at Max and said the accident had pushed his tooth back into the gum. I could not believe it but one of his two first baby teeth was pushed back inside his gum. I wanted to deny that the tooth had ever come through and difficult though it may be to believe I genuinely believed that the tooth had never come through. For me this was a classic case of cognitive dissonance. In fact it heralded a turning point in my life and was the start of my psychological studies. I could not believe that I had honestly thought that the tooth had not come through. It was only because I trusted my husband completely that I could start to look at what had happened and marvel at how my brain desperately wanted to present another story.

You may be thinking: why do I need to know all this stuff? What I want are the keys to better relationships to improve my career and ability to manage people more effectively, not a treatise on my childhood programming. Yet the most important and difficult fact to grasp is that who you are today all started in childhood and everything about us stems back to childhood and always will unless we do this work of understanding.

The fact is your essence was built in those early days and what happened in your childhood substantially impacts your relationships today. We are focusing on it here so that you can understand yourself better.

When we can understand ourselves better all our relationships flow more easily. When we have a clearer appreciation of who we are and where we came from we will also understand others more easily. The payoff of this work is that it makes managing others much easier, particularly if interactions aren't going to plan and situations start to spiral out of control.

Every time we feel an extreme or intense emotion such as being very angry, frustrated, intolerant or wanting to plot revenge, our crocodile is in charge. A sobering thought if we think of all the times in the day when we can feel so out of sorts with another.

What a delight if we could choose to engage our rational thinking brain rather than reacting emotively from the crocodile brain. It would certainly give us the power or upper hand when things become volatile.

In chapter 3 we talked about how once the unconscious has made up its mind about something it doesn't want to change and looks to find any evidence and justification to support its world view, while quietly ignoring any facts that may contradict it. This is what we are going to explore in depth with this fifth key understanding.

Our early self holds the key to our current self

Let's briefly recap what we know about our earliest self.

We know that when we were born our unconscious ruled. It is the oldest part of our brain (crocodile brain) and its main purpose was, and is, to ensure we survive.

Little crocodiles are not particularly social so we had to be socialised by our parents to ensure that society survived and did not turn to anarchy, which it would have if we hadn't all been socialised. Our instinctive desire as little crocodiles is to take what we want, when we want it, with no thought of anyone else. When we couldn't get what we wanted we manipulated, schemed, bullied and fought. Remember all we were concerned about was survival and getting our 3Ss satisfied. Being part of a family, however, it was vital that we were socialised; so we were taught the family rules. Some rules were overt but many were covert. Little by little we were programmed with many behaviours, values and ideas. That programming formed our blueprint, one full of beliefs and drivers that are probably not even ours if we stopped long enough to examine them. All those rules, injunctions and beliefs were imprinted before our brain was developed enough to be able to differentiate between those that we may agree with and those we don't.

Socialisation

With that in mind, let's move to the fifth key.

During our socialisation process we came to understand that it was wrong to steal, to bully, to fight and all those other 'bad' things we were told we were doing. We had to learn quickly how to be 'good' children because otherwise our 3Ss were threatened and we did not feel safe or loved.

We know from our brain structure that we are hardwired to be profoundly relational; we thrive when we work together. The fear of not getting the attention and love from our parents or caregivers was very strong. All this made us much more susceptible to being moulded into a socially acceptable shape.

However our basic instincts did not magically disappear because our crocodile brain is our brain's foundation. We did not suddenly turn into perfect little cherubs, and being smart, we learned to adapt. We learned to hide the 'naughty' parts of ourselves so we would still get the love and attention we needed. We learnt that if we didn't behave and hide the 'bad' parts we would usually get punished. That threatened our core need for survival.

The result of all this was that we became 'adapted' (nicely programmed) children. Our free crocodile child was educated to fit into the system. We learnt to obey the rules to a greater or lesser extent. We accepted that others knew best. Consequently, and here is the sad, disappointing part, we absorbed the idea that there were parts of us that were bad or unacceptable. Those parts didn't just magically disappear. Either they were suppressed and went underground, into our unconscious, stored away only to come out when we thought others were not watching; or maybe cognitive dissonance enabled us to forget we even had 'bad' parts at all.

Our secret self

The sad thing about being civilised is that, although it is probably "humankind's greatest achievement, it culls out the characteristics that are dangerous to the smooth functioning of our ideals. Anyone who does not go through this process remains a 'primitive' and can have no place in a civilised society. We are all born whole but somehow the culture demands that we live out only part of our nature and refuse other parts of our inheritance."[20]

We have all suppressed things we don't like about ourselves or think are unacceptable. We even go as far as disguising it from ourselves – for example: I don't want to share my chocolate, but I don't want to acknowledge to myself that I'm mean or that I want the largest slice of pie; I don't return the extra money the shop assistant gave me when she gave me too much change, but I'm not going to recognize that it could be looked on as taking advantage of another; I lie about the amount of alcohol I have drunk when the police stop me on the road; I tell work I am sick when really I am just tired and want a day off; I lie when my girlfriend asks me if she looks fat in her dress; I deceive when I say the cheque must have got lost in the post because I definitely sent it when a bill is outstanding. And the list goes on. We have all done it. It may flash through our

---

[20] Dr Robert A Johnson, *Owning your own shadow.*

mind that our behaviour is not the best but we justify it to ourselves saying everyone does it.

All of these hidden traits, that are instinctively part of human nature, get suppressed down in our unconscious. Perhaps at some point they helped our survival as a species, but they are now generally considered socially unacceptable.

I have called all our 'bad' parts our 'secret self', which as we now know is buried in our unconscious. (One of the founders of modern psychology, famous psychiatrist Carl Jung, called this the shadow, but for ease of understanding I called it the secret self.)

In effect we disown our secret self as in the examples above. This learning to disown our secret self started as young children because back then there was so much information we had to absorb that we couldn't or didn't have the physical ability to deal with difficult or painful information. It takes energy, time and sophisticated thought processes to self-reflect on our behaviour, which as kids we didn't have the resources to do. Now as adults it still takes a lot of time and energy to think through our behaviour carefully and most of us don't bother.

However it also takes a lot of energy to keep our secret self hidden or suppressed, to present the 'perfect' façade. Our secret self "often has an energy potential nearly as great as that of our ego," says noted author and Jungian analyst, Robert Johnson. [21]

---

[21] Dr Robert A Johnson, *Owning your own shadow.*

When hidden traits emerge unintentionally and cause chaos

How often have we seen high profile people, who have worked really hard to get to those heights by being model members of society, come crashing down because they have lied about their behaviour?

If we look at some of the well-known US politicians such as Bill Clinton, Eliot Spitzer (former governor of New York) and recently Anthony Weiner being brought undone by trying to hide their humanness under a cloak of perfection.

We often see the same thing in business – the Bernard Madoff Ponzi scheme, he promised wonders, yet he was actually a sophisticated crook.

In the above cases their secret self came out, as it did with the great cyclist Lance Armstrong and his continual denial of the use of performance enhancing drugs until he was eventually exposed. Martha Stewart, a household name in the US, was brought undone by insider trading. History is littered with people who have fallen short of the expectations they have worked so hard to build.

On the corporate front we have seen the spectacular collapse of Enron due to a painstakingly planned accounting fraud made by Arthur Anderson, where thousands of employees and investors saw their savings lost. In Australia we saw the collapse of HIH Insurance after many false and misleading statements were made by Rodney Adler. There was the Lockheed bribery scandal and the Walmart bribery scandal, not to mention Lehman Brothers, Fannie Mae, Freddie Mac, Merrill Lynch, and a myriad others – all trying to appear to be the perfect organisation yet riddled with unacknowledged imperfection that eventually bought them down.

Back to the personal, secretly we probably all want to be thought of as close to perfect and have the accompanying façade; however we are all human and inevitably fallible.

So why do we strive for perfection? Again this is our unconscious and programming coming into play – if we are exceptional we think we are safe and often work extremely hard to be thought of as wonderful. However, as in the cases above, their secret selves eventually emerged to leave a trail of destruction pain and chaos. When we don't acknowledge our less pleasant but very human characteristics our secret self will come out to play and does so as soon as our guard is down.

We are now getting to the cutting edge of why relationships go wrong

Operating at an unconscious level we find others to carry the energy of our disowned, suppressed parts. This sounds extraordinary, but this is what we do. And what makes it even more extraordinary is that it happens out of our conscious awareness. We call this phenomenon **projection**. When we become aware of projection it is easy to spot.

The start of projection

Here's a quick example of projection and we cover this topic in more detail in the next chapter.

Joe is jealous of Adam's new car but doesn't want to admit this. He has been conditioned to believe that jealousy is not a nice trait, so he says to Adam, "how wonderful, you are lucky and you deserve it, I'd love a car like that". Sounds friendly on the surface and Joe is partially genuine when he says it, yet every time he looks at the car he feels angry muttering under his breath: "can't think why he gets a car like that while I am so much better at my job than him. I should be getting paid more so I can get a car like that." What's happening? Joe may be pleased for Adam at some level but he is envious and his self-talk puts Adam down. Joe is feeling resentment that he is not getting paid more. Beneath the surface bitterness is starting to grow which in due course could contaminate the relationship between the two men.

If Joe had been more aware he would have owned his jealousy, acknowledged it, and instead of denigrating Adam, allowed himself to feel envy. We all feel envy or have felt it at some stage and that's normal. The pitfall or trap is what we do about the feeling. If we take a minute to face what is making us feel angry, upset or irritated, we can acknowledge it and then decide whether it is helpful or unhelpful. We don't need to find fault with the innocent party who has a fancy car or end up resenting our boss or our jobs because we want to be paid more.

*Joe has **projected his discomfort** onto Adam and his boss and disguises this by believing he is a victim, life is unfair.*

Focusing on Adam and his boss stops him being pro-active and keeps him stuck in the past.

....

Another brief example: Miranda hates people who cheat the system. Her programming has been that this is wicked so she is very attuned to spotting people who can rort a scheme and generally will report them. She told company authorities when a co-worker claimed expenses he had not actually made. She prides herself on being scrupulously honest. However recently she attended a workshop where at the end of the two days there was a celebratory dinner to which partners were invited and their dinner had to be paid for by an honesty system. Miranda brought her partner to the dinner yet forgot to pay for him!

To recognise behaviour and other people's emotions we need to have felt them to some degree ourselves. To recognise murder does not mean that you are a murderer and can kill people; however chances are you will have killed a mosquito landing on you or a spider or a cockroach in your cupboard. So while you are not a murderer you can kill. What we see in others will always be there to some degree in ourselves. **If you spot it you've got it or at least degrees of it.** And that is fine. It all goes wrong when we don't admit it.

Miranda was acting as a policewoman, reporting her co-worker and being scandalised that he could be dishonest; yet she was being dishonest herself in not paying for her partner at the dinner, just sneaking him in. Yes, the scale of the offence may be different but not what underlies her action. Miranda was projecting her own disowned ability of 'cheating and being dishonest' onto her co-worker. She then covered it from herself by her righteous indignation because she could not accept that she also had the ability to be dishonest. Yet, she too cheated the system. To give Miranda her due, she was no doubt totally unaware of what she was doing.

Can you see how people project? The first step is to suppress the traits that society deems unacceptable. They drop into our unconscious, out of conscious awareness, but these traits don't disappear, they are just hidden. In order to hide them or their urges, we are much more likely to point them out in other people and thus take the heat off ourselves. If others consider Miranda honest and righteous, they would never suspect her of being a cheat herself. She would no doubt have a hundred excuses as to why she rorted the system by not paying for her partner. The trap is that in justifying her behaviour to herself she avoids having to admit that she too has the ability to cheat and be dishonest.

Chapter Recap

Our childhood programming taught us that there were many parts of ourselves that were unacceptable – the lying, cheating, bullying, aggressive parts – and in order to be loved and get the attention we needed they had to be suppressed and hidden away.

We were socialised.

These disowned parts didn't just go away as they are fundamental to our crocodile brain and underlie all our human characteristics. They also helped us to survive.

Collectively, these behaviours, traits and characteristics, became our 'Secret Self'.

It takes energy to cover these disowned aspects of ourselves so we find another to carry the aspects of our self that we don't think are acceptable. This is called **projection.**

When you spot another's flaws, know that you've got that same flaw or at least degrees of it.

If you are aware of this very human behaviour, admit it and accept it – you will have choice about entertaining and using that behaviour.

Your journey

Think of characteristics in others that you dislike, perhaps by bringing to mind someone you really dislike.

Can you acknowledge aspects of yourself that might have some similarity to those you dislike?

Chapter 7

The sixth key: to avoid looking at our own imperfect characteristics we focus on others' faults – PROJECTION

This is where all the psychological underpinning starts to come together and the work gets more difficult. It takes courage to take this well-known psychological principle on board and to admit that you project. Let's be really clear about this – we all project and we project 24 x 7. We project because we view the world through our own lenses, which have been built up of our own experiences, expectations and beliefs.

If you choose to read on you will be stepping through the Looking Glass as in Alice in Wonderland and there is no stepping back. Once you understand the principle it behoves you to take responsibility. While we are unaware we just keep going our merry way projecting here, there and everywhere, seeing all the faults in others that we don't believe we have or are even capable of having. As they say, ignorance is bliss. The downside of that ignorance is that our relationships suffer and often cause us considerable grief.

Before we dive into the mechanics of projection it is important to realise that it stems from an unconscious need we all share. At a deep level we all want to be loved, cherished, validated and thought to be wonderful! We would also like to be looked after 24 x 7, as long as that does not interfere with whatever we want to do.

Imagine a perfect person who did everything you wanted, who took complete care of you, with none of the downside of having to think of what their needs might be, sort of like an intelligent loving slave! The bad news is that this scenario is completely idealistic. However, that does not prevent us striving to get it and, worse still, continuing to look for it even though our thinking rational neo-cortex knows better. This very basic underlying human need to be loved, cherished and be in relationships with perfect others contaminates all our interactions to some degree unless we can pull it into check.

The ideal parent

For a moment let's imagine we are children and look at what we want from the ideal parent:

- Loves us unconditionally
- Overlooks our faults
- Even better, doesn't see any faults
- Is not harsh with us
- Agrees with what we want
- Praises us often
- Is fair

Anyone disagree with that?

The ideal child

Now let's imagine we are parents. What would we want from the ideal child?

- Always obedient
- Always loving
- Always achieves
- Enhances our reputation as a parent in every way!

Wow, wouldn't that make parenting a breeze?

The ideal partner

Would your ideal partner look something like this?

- Loves me passionately and says he/she always will
- Says I'm the most important thing in the world to him/her
- Compliments me about my looks, body, personality, intelligence, sex appeal, charm and everything else about me
- Is willing to drop everything to do whatever I want
- Is prepared to put my needs above his/hers
- Amuses me, entertains me and gives me space when I need it

Wouldn't that be perfect? Could perhaps eventually get a little dull ...

The ideal employee

Let's look at the ideal employee:

- Is always enthusiastic and prepared to do any extra work that may be necessary
- Is intelligent
- Takes initiative and comes up with good ideas
- Is careful and doesn't stuff up
- Is responsible
- Is always of a cheerful, happy disposition
- Doesn't spend any time on personal matters
- Is loyal and doesn't gossip with other employees
- Makes me look good as a boss
- Is good value for what I pay them

Perfect if I'm the boss ...

The ideal boss

How about the ideal boss?

- He/she is very understanding and kind
- Understands that I have a life outside work

- Wants me to do interesting, stimulating work, not boring, repetitive old stuff

- Wants to give me responsibility when I want it, but is prepared to take the rap if I stuff up

- Wants me to take initiative and have autonomy, but again will take responsibility if it doesn't work out

- Rewards me in many different ways: money, praise, time off, good trips etc

- Is always fair

Nice ...

Wouldn't life be just perfect if others could provide the above? However unless we can be all of the above to everybody 24 x 7 we are just plain dreaming! And that is the sad reality of it. So now, knowing that we are not all perfect, let's look at what we do to cover our disappointment that life doesn't give us the above.

The oldest trick in the book

We project. Projection is the tool we use to identify those traits in others that we do not want to see in ourselves. Projection comes from a deep, largely unconscious level of fear that if people see our displeasing traits they will not like us and at some level reject us. (3Ss not being met.)

Projection is constantly flashing signposts at us. We will know it is either occurring or ready to occur when we feel strongly about someone, or more particularly when we actively dislike a particular characteristic someone is displaying. Perhaps when you feel reactive about the following behaviours: lying, manipulation, arrogance, bullying, coercing, blaming, criticising, laziness, conceit, dictatorial, cunning, sabotaging, lustiness and the list goes on and on, projection may be coming into play. For example the adulterous wife accuses her husband of having an affair. The lazy husband accuses his wife of being indolent. The bully accuses another of harassment. A pacifist says he could never kill and then gets the insecticide to destroy the spider.

Just think for a moment about the attributes you hate the most. This intense dislike of particular traits usually signposts your own predisposition towards them. The greater the emotional response to a trait the more resonance it has with us personally. In an ideal world all emotions are quite neutral. What I mean about the neutrality of an emotion is that it assumes a quality of 'just is'.

Let's look at arrogance. Imagine your departmental head seems to swagger about and sits in his corner office with the great view and seems too busy and important to talk to you except when he absolutely has to. He often seems to have an air of superiority. Recognise the characteristic?

What's the opposite of arrogance? Perhaps humility, modesty and self-diffidence. Someone who doesn't put on airs and graces and is humble and certainly doesn't big-note himself.

If we put these characteristics on a continuum they would probably look like this:

Subservient ⇒ Humility

or

Unassumingly Confident ⇒ Arrogance

Ideally we would find ourselves in the middle of the continuum, just quietly confident in our abilities. Yet at times we can feel humble in the face of brilliance or great creativity; and in different circumstances sometimes we may feel our own wisdom and experience and move towards the arrogant end of the spectrum. If we are more aware of arrogance than humility that is a signpost for us that at times we possibly err on the arrogant side. Most of us secretly want to be better than the next person because that's our crocodile brain at play.

On the personal front let's look at love, which has so many different shades. It can be tempestuous like passionate romantic love, or deep and quiet like you have for your grandmother. If we put love on a continuum as below ...

Indifference ⇒ Love ⇒ Grand Passion

... we see indifference on one end of the spectrum and grand passion on the other. Our feelings move along the continuum. For instance, grand passion will slowly fade back towards the middle as no one can sustain the demands of grand passion for very long. (Grand passion is expecting our every need to be met by another.

Unfortunately it does not last as we slowly realise our great love has his or her own faults, needs and desires and can't give us everything we want all the time – not to mention the energetic cost of grand passion.)

Of course there are different levels of love but when it feels comfortable and easy our emotional response is relaxed. When the emotional response is relaxed it is not signalling projection.

Hate is a different cup of tea.

$$Love \Rightarrow Indifference \Rightarrow Hate$$

Hate generates significant energy; there is nothing quiet or passive about it. It is not a relaxed emotional response that 'just is.' It does not sit in the middle of an emotional continuum. When we feel strong emotions like hate we are looking at some level of projection.

When we use substantial energy to deny some trait, behaviour or characteristic know that projection is present. We need to recognise that what we are seeing we are capable of. It is part of our secret self that is alive and flourishing. As famous spiritual teacher and author Eckhart Tolle says: "Anything that you resent and strongly react to in another is also in you".[22]

Craig was feeling depressed and inadequate. A few months earlier, he had started a new job, working as a sales manager for Martin. To start with their relationship went well, but gradually Craig felt Martin was putting

---

[22] Eckhart Tolle, *A New Earth: Awakening to your life's purpose.*

him under enormous pressure to get the sales up. He was feeling anxious about being able to deliver because the products weren't as good as he had been led to believe. Craig didn't want to complain in case Martin thought he was making excuses and was a lousy salesman. Then Craig realised that Martin himself was under substantial pressure from the chairman, to produce good sales figures, and Martin's own job was on the line. Craig realised that Martin was relying on him to deliver those results to protect his job.

What is going on here? Martin is projecting his anxiety about his own job prospects onto Craig. Meanwhile, Craig is feeling unhappy and uncertain under the huge pressure. He doesn't want to tell the truth about the product line in case he is thought inadequate in his role as a salesman. He no longer has confidence in his boss, Martin, nor does he have confidence in the product he is trying to sell. This has a negative impact on potential clients, who, picking up on his energy, aren't motivated to buy. A negative spiral has been set up, largely based on projection.

Martin unconsciously wants to blame Craig for poor sales, yet that's not where the problem lies. It is compounded because Martin, although the managing director, is not a good communicator and is out of touch with his people. Although Martin is aware of problems with the product he doesn't want to address them because the chairman is judging his performance. Without consciously realising it he is hoping that Craig can produce magic and prevent the whole situation unravelling. He blames others for being inadequate in their jobs when he himself is not performing adequately. Unconsciously Martin hopes that

> *Craig is seen to be more inadequate than he is so he has a buffer against dismissal.*

How could this have been handled differently? If, as soon as the relationship started to sour, there had been honest communication about the situation and the root causes of everyone's anxiety, it could have been different.

This lack of openness is going on to some extent in all organisations, from the simplest company to the boards of every major corporation. If people could be more self-confident they would be able to talk about what was going on for them rather than protect an image. Imagine how much more effective we'd all be if we could talk openly about our concerns without fear of being judged inadequate.

A general rule of thumb to understand projection is: 'if you spot it you've probably got it' or at least tendencies towards it. We are all in exactly the same boat, we have faults and we are able to see the faults in others. It is fine to see that someone is lying or cheating as long as we have the awareness to know that there have been times when we too have lied or cheated. Someone who is law-abiding will notice people who break the law and will be quick to judge them. Our secret self, all those traits that we disown in ourselves, jump out when we can see them in another and we love to point out their flaws. It makes us feel better and helps us keep our perfect façade intact, or so we think.

Malcolm was quick to find fault with Anne, particularly her lack of attention to detail, which he felt was sloppiness. He used any opportunity to point out her flaws to whoever would listen, from the receptionist, her direct reports, to her manager. Anne was on the same management level as Malcolm and he saw her as competition so consciously felt threatened and was trying to undermine her. While others could see what he was doing Malcolm was unaware that his behaviour was being noted and working against him. In fact the sloppiness he was busy pointing out in Anne was being reflected in his own work because he was so busy monitoring Anne.

Projection is the oldest trick in the book and has been part of mankind's armoury since we first walked on the earth. Jesus made one famous comment about projection when he said, "Cast out the log in your own eye, so that you can see the mote in your brother's eye" (Matthew 7:5 and Luke 6:42).

Awareness of our projections, like the secret self, is a portal into part of our unconscious. It is important to understand it well, because it plays a huge role in all our relationships, as we will see in the seventh and last key understanding.

Projection is not all bad

Projection is not all bad and negative. We project onto people we admire. We may envy some of their characteristics without realising that we have similar characteristics. When we recognise creative genius in another know that we have a degree of that wonderful characteristic – an amazing thought. The traits may not be as well developed but nevertheless they are there, otherwise how would we recognise them?

So when we admire intelligence, grace or charm appreciate that by identifying these traits in others we have the same attributes to some extent and can embrace and celebrate them as part of us.

Projection also serves a valuable purpose as a protective, defensive coping mechanism. It takes the aspects of our secret self that we cannot accept and sees them in others. The more we lack insight and awareness into our own behavioural characteristics the more we will project. It allows us to cope when we are not ready to confront our own traits, (perhaps as a first step to embracing them). Becoming aware of our strong emotions and setting aside some time to reflect is a big step forward. We may not have the resources, time, and courage to deal completely with every situation, so projection lets us set aside certain issues for the time being while signposting the situation.

Let's look at the following example. Alan has been asked to give a quote for an IT service for a large chain of departmental stores. He has underestimated the complexity of the quote and rushing to finish it in time he realises that some key elements have been forgotten which will dramatically impact the costing. As Alan is realising this he is immediately taken back to the last time he rushed a quote and the job was accepted; however Alan lost money on the project. In this instance, as he thinks about the current quote, he is projecting his frustration and anxiety from the last situation on this current quote and feels a sense of foreboding. But that was then and Alan is in a different situation now, particularly if he gives himself a moment to think about what is going on emotionally. However anxiety is starting to overwhelm him and the feeling of being late on the quote sends him into a tailspin. If Alan could have stopped and thought objectively about what signals his anxiety was sending he could have prevented the tailspin. From the neuroscience perspective once in the tailspin his neocortex was starting to shut down and rational thinking was going out of the window.

Our bodies send us signals

Our bodies send us vital signals. When there is emotional heat or reactivity our body is waving a red flag at us, such as in the example above. Or sometimes we get hold of an idea and go around and around with it, particularly if we think we are right and the other is wrong. Remember how our crocodile brain wants to be right. The trick is to tear ourselves away from our own moralistic soapbox long enough to observe ourselves objectively.

Personally I find that my moralistic soapbox is a comfortable place to be. I go round and round justifying my actions to myself. Emotions and physical reactions give us the opportunity to reflect and signal a valuable insight coming from our crocodile brain. I call these emotional signals triggers. They will usually prompt a bodily reaction, i.e. anxiety or discomfort. We may focus on our anxiety about something or a particular situation and avoid looking at what purpose our anxiety is serving, what underlies our anxiety.

The same applies when we are feeling uncomfortable. To avoid doing the detective work of investigating what is going on at a deeper level we will come up with diversionary tactics such as keeping ourselves extremely busy so there is no time for self-reflection. We may engage in addictive behaviour such as alcohol, drugs, gambling, sex, sport, and the list goes on. We may divert our attention by diving into work, turning on the television, talking to our friends about what is going on for them, eat, immerse ourselves in the computer or with a book.

Our diversionary distracting tactics are endless. I compulsively clean when I am feeling uncomfortable. We are extremely skilled at avoiding looking at what is behind our own emotional states.

What you resist persists

You've probably heard the expression, what you resist persists. This is because everything in our world is built around a dynamic tension between opposing forces. There is a balance between rest and activity, between expansion and contraction, summer and winter, night and day and so on. When you think of your uncomfortable feelings, or your difficult relationships, you create a dynamic tension by wanting them to improve or change. Wanting something implies that you do not already have it, so we create tension. For example, you have some money yet you want more. The focus is not on the money you have but on what you do not have. While you continue to think about what you do not have you make it a bigger issue. It becomes all about what you do not have rather than what you do have.

What you resist persists, because you continue to ruminate about it. You actively try to achieve something and by giving it more and more of your attention you fuel the issue and it gets worse. One solution is to focus on what you want to achieve with the money; what you want to use it for, the car, the holiday or the house etc. This shifts the focus to being pro-active rather than a victim of circumstance.

In the case of a relationship, try to focus on the aspects that do work and not the ones that don't work. Perhaps try and focus on what you would like to see, instead of all the bad and unsatisfying aspects. The trick with relationships is to isolate the particular characteristic or characteristics you are finding difficult about the other person, then go back through your memory banks and see if you can find the earliest example of those same characteristics irritating or causing you anxiety or distress.

It may be way back in childhood or at school or it may be a more recent situation. It is highly likely that the crocodile part of your brain, remembering the earlier situation, is signalling danger and is projecting the outcome of that earlier incident onto what is happening now in the current difficult relationship.

In building a business imagine how it looks as a successful enterprise rather than focusing on all the negatives, the poor performance of the employees, the lack of sufficient cash flow, the poor market conditions etc – again the list will be endless. This takes discipline, as it is easier for our brain to focus on the negative.

Steve Jobs wouldn't have built Apple if all he saw were the obstacles ahead of him. The same would apply to Richard Branson. Tolle says: "acknowledging the good you already have in your life is the foundation for all abundance".[23]

Polarities are neutral

These polarities are the driving force of all action. They are neither good nor bad; they just are. However, by creating the polarity, for instance in wanting discomfort to go away, you are actually creating a tension that enables you to feel the discomfort more intensely. If you can allow the discomfort to be there, to sit in it, it will subside. For most of us the need to avoid unpleasant feelings is so strong that to stay within the discomfort may seem a strange idea. In today's world we want and expect instant gratification and resolution. However, if we stay with the tension and tolerate those moments of chaos and confusion, we can generally find a more profound and lasting solution. When we are feeling discomfort we usually fish around for someone or something to project onto as that allows us not to feel our discomfort so acutely. Instead of avoiding feeling discomfort and projecting onto others, it is healthier to

---

23 Eckhart Tolle, *A New Earth: Awakening to your life's purpose.*

allow the feeling to be there, think about it, accept that it is how you feel right at this moment, and then allow it to pass.

Acknowledging the feeling enables it to pass more easily. It is as if it has been heard. It becomes unhealthy when we can't stop ourselves thinking about a particular negative emotion and it becomes an obsessive loop.

When we sit in our feelings and accept them it: a) gives us the space to accept ourselves and forgive ourselves, and b) gives us the opportunity to gain perspective and choose our actions carefully rather than have knee-jerk reactions to rid ourselves of discomfort. Sitting with the feeling, in ambiguity, can allow different perspectives to open up.

Ian is fed up that his boss is not coming back to him with feedback about his proposal and the delay worries him. When he stops to think what's going on in his boss's working life he can see how stressed his boss is and that awareness alleviates Ian's own anxiety. Ian realises that the reason his boss hasn't come back to him is probably because he isn't really thinking about Ian at all. As Ian thought about this his own personal situation crossed his mind, he knew he was fed up with his home situation. He was feeling nagged by his wife, feeling he has to be at her beck and call, especially during the weekends. As he stayed with his anger and frustration instead of getting mad with his wife, it occurred to him that his wife demanding his attention was perhaps her way of wanting him close at weekends. He was surprised at this thought

---

> *and talked to his wife to try and confirm if this was correct. When she affirmed this for him he felt differently and agreed to do things together for some of the time but said that he also needed to have his own time. Their marital situation improved dramatically. If only all partnership dynamics could be so easily solved!*

What we face dissipates

You can add to the phrase, 'what we resist persists' with 'what we face dissipates.' Our fears arise from what we do not confront, not from what we examine. When we look fully and deeply at the source of the discomfort and the fear driving it, the fear loses some of its intensity and power. The truth is that there is nothing within us that can hurt us. After all whatever is inside us is what we have already felt and judged. It is our fear of re-experiencing our own feelings that keeps us trapped. This is an important point and bears repeating: The truth is that there is nothing within us that can hurt us. What is inside us is what we have already felt and judged. It is our fear of re-experiencing our own feelings that keeps us trapped.

> *Duncan was retrenched. This was terrifying as he had accumulated huge debts due to his drug problem and his landlord had given him notice for late rent payments. Without a job he was in a dire situation with no one to fall back on for help and nowhere to live. He had to live on the street until he found work again. Eventually he found work and painstakingly rebuilt his life. However he was so ashamed of that period of his life that he shut it away*

> *and never talked about it. When he was able to acknowledge his earlier irresponsible behaviour and talk about it he realised that he had learnt an invaluable lesson and instead of shutting that period away he used it as an illustration of what can happen, to help and inspire others. The energy he used to keep it hidden was now liberated and he felt clearer and better about his life.*

Often we will say, "I don't want to think about that again, it's over and forgotten." Yet when we face our fears and the situations that we do not like we don't necessarily find immediate resolution, but if we can be courageous enough to sit within the tension something will inevitably shift. Just by experiencing what we are feeling we have taken the first step to resolution.

The next step is to name what we are feeling because that helps us regain control and a little distance. Then as we give ourselves some time the solution invariably unfolds and becomes clearer. At that stage we are well on our way to resolving the situation. Often a night's sleep will enable us to see things differently. We gain a different perspective. However we won't necessarily resolve everything overnight; it can often take weeks, months or sometimes years. So it is important to be gentle with yourself and know that you are holding a tension that could be projection – either your projection onto another or their projection onto you.

When we are temporarily obsessed

A quick jump to the neuroscience: when we ruminate about things too much, we risk becoming temporarily obsessed, lose our perspective and fail to act logically.

David Rock[24] tells us that if we continue to think too much about a particular incident we risk overwhelming our limbic system and our brain does not work well. We have to divert ourselves to do something else, go for a walk or work on something completely different and when we come back to look at the problem it usually looks very different. We change our focus, refresh our brain and free it from the lockdown of a particular mode of thinking.

When we start to obsess we have gone into a state of fear. We may not be aware of this on a conscious level but our crocodile is certainly aware and our level of cortisol, or stress hormone, has probably flooded our body. When cortisol is elevated our neo-cortex starts to shut down, waiting for the flight or fight reflex to kick in, so we are less able to think creatively. In fact we are hardly thinking at all.

If we are able to sit in discomfort and self-reflect we can take comfort in knowing that we are developing and changing our brain for the better.

---

[24] Dr David Rock, *Your Brain at Work.*

Chapter Recap

We all want to be loved, validated and looked after 24 x 7. Ideally we would like our 3Ss met without any effort on our part. When we don't get that we feel disillusioned and project onto others.

Projection is the oldest trick in the human armoury – it's not our fault; it is someone else's fault. Shifting blame and taking the focus off ourselves is human nature.

Projection plays havoc with our relationships.

Once we understand the concept we can become aware of when we are projecting by looking for emotional and physical triggers.

Projection is not all negative. The positive qualities we see in others we also have, as long as we give ourselves permission to own them.

Identifying our projections helps us understand our programming. And awareness of our projections is a valuable portal into our unconscious.

When we feel emotionally reactive we have the opportunity to go deeper and learn more about ourselves. Knowing more gives us choice.

Most of the time we are adept at using many different diversionary tactics to avoid attending to our own bodily signposts.

What we resist persists.

What we face dissipates.

When we start to think obsessively we stop thinking creatively – in fact we aren't thinking at all!

Your journey

In the exercises in the last chapter you thought about a person you disliked and perhaps were able to recognise that you had some ability to either recognise or act on some of those characteristics.

Now let's consider the positive aspects of projection. Can you identify in yourself some of the traits that you admire in another?

Can you identify situations where you have become emotionally reactive and work out what was triggered in you and why? (This is not about the other person and their actions. It is solely about you and which of your beliefs was impacted and what fear was your crocodile brain reacting to?)

Chapter 8

The seventh key: our projections influence the way we think about others and that in turn affects our behaviour

So let's stop for a moment and do a brief recap.

Brain: 3 levels of the brain

- Crocodile (manifests through the unconscious)
- Horse (manifests through the unconscious)
- Neo-cortex

Unconscious:

- What it does, how it works
- How it is programmed
- What happens when it feels threatened

Beliefs:

- Initially stem from programming of the unconscious by parents
- Rarely changes in a lifetime unless underlying beliefs are examined
- Largely accepted as the status quo

Secret Self:

- Secret self – represses so-called unattractive qualities

- Not acknowledged, nevertheless very human

Projection:

- The secret self's weapon

- The things we dislike or don't acknowledge in ourselves we see in others

- Become our triggers

- Tells us about our unconscious beliefs and motivations

We know that projection is at play when we are emotionally triggered. If we can stop and think 'my secret self is trying to say something here, let's listen', this will cut the behaviourial loop before we project outwards. This allows us to liberate trapped energy.

Liberating our energy

It takes energy to protect our 'perfect façade.' It means we have to be continually aware of how we are coming across to others. It means that we are attempting to mind-read and often second-guess ourselves, which is tiring and time consuming. It also means we are not in the 'now' but in the past or future. "Make the NOW the primary focus of your life," says Tolle, because the present moment is all we have.[25]

When we are in the past we are trying to work out how we came across, and if we are in the future we wonder how others will think, neither of which bodes well for sound relationships. Successful interactions work best when we are fully in the moment, concentrating on the other. We connect get resonance and both parties feel seen and heard.

Using our secret self to gain awareness

Recognising our disowned secret self when we feel emotional distress or reactivity is a fundamental key to sustaining healthy relationships. When we take the time to reflect we gain self-awareness, enabling us to know ourselves better. We begin to recognise some of our programming and check with ourselves whether it is OK or if we need a software update. Awareness gives us conscious choices, not choices springing from our unconscious wanting to protect our 3Ss. For instance, when we feel threatened many of us respond reactively by being devious, manipulative or dishonest etc. It is unlikely we would use those behaviours if we were making them in full consciousness.

Carmen is a departmental head and intends applying for the CEO position, as with her boss leaving, it's becoming available. She has been working for the organisation for twenty years and knows it extremely well. However as she

---

[25] Eckhart Tolle, *A New Earth: Awakening to your life's purpose.*

makes her intention known she is quietly told there is no point in applying, as she wouldn't get the job, which embitters Carmen. When the new CEO starts in his role Carmen is already offside even though she doesn't know him, and she starts to undermine him. Soon tensions are running high. To cope Carmen co-opts one of her direct reports into siding with her against the CEO. The direct report is in a difficult situation. She wants to support Carmen but obviously doesn't want to alienate the CEO, and to cope with her own anxiety she gossips with her co-workers which slowly demoralises the organisation. The whole situation is turning toxic and it isn't the new CEO's fault. We can see how Carmen's vindictiveness is having a detrimental effect. If Carmen was more aware of her own anger and disappointment she might have made different choices but her secret self was running her show.

Let's turn our attention to the CEO, what does he do in this situation? Having been in the organisation for twenty years, Carmen has knowledge that he would like to tap into but he can't put up with her undermining him. While it may create waves in the company it is important that he asserts his authority, as a new CEO. He confronts Carmen who realises that she has to make a choice. Either she stops the behaviour and keeps her job or she leaves. It is similar to disciplining and teaching a child. Carmen has to be taught respect and find a way to deal with her own disappointment.

Most of the time we want to disown our secret self. Rather than do this, start to welcome it as an invaluable tool for increasing your self-awareness. When we can see our own fallibilities clearly, even if we never act on them – eg, I hate meanness and can see it like a flashing beacon in others yet acknowledge that at times I can be mean – we become slower to criticise others. When we are more self-aware we are aware of others and become slower to criticise and judge. We become more compassionate, understanding people, which can only be beneficial.

The biggest benefit occurs when we become less judgemental, more compassionate and more understanding of ourselves.

Throughout this book we have covered why and how our secret self has developed. We know it is fundamentally a protective tool and understand that unless it is brought into check, it can be extraordinarily destructive because unconsciously we usually want to find someone else to be the 'bad' guy. In crocodile terms we want to be the top crocodile or nearer the top than the bottom of the pecking order, so we can feel safe and secure, or at least better than other crocodiles.

In your journey you are becoming aware that if you take the easy route and suppress discomfort as your preferred way of coping you only obtain short-term benefits. This strategy can and usually does sabotage relationships and in the process deprives you of choice and empowerment. When we are unaware we have limited choices and our behaviour springs from that primitive, unconscious, self-protective place which invariably finds another as a target.

You now have awareness and choice and already have turned a major corner towards happier, successful, satisfying relationships.

Dad comes home from work after a difficult day and stumbles over kids' toys at the front door. He yells at the kids to pick up their toys. Mum gets defensive; after all, the children are children and they have a right to play in their home. A few minutes later the eldest child is picking a fight with the youngest for being so messy and the youngest in frustration goes over to the sleeping cat and yanks her tail!

Can you see the pattern? Can you see how the family are projecting their frustrations onto each other? First the father onto the children after his difficult day, then the eldest child blames the younger one and finally projects her discomfort by plaguing the cat.

The scenario is familiar. Projection is at work; we all try to get rid of our anxiety and frustration somewhere.

Let's take that example further: Dad is yelling and Mum is getting defensive, thinking he's unreasonable. 'We are quietly getting on with life and he comes home with his bad mood and the contented energy in the house has just evaporated.' Later that evening Dad picking up Mum's vibe asks what's wrong and he gets met with a frosty comment 'nothing'. The rot has started, distance is established, Dad sulks and the situation goes from bad to worse. It is easy to see how these simple little projections have influenced the way Mum thought about Dad, and

---

their behaviour towards each other. This type of interaction erodes our relationships over time.

If Dad could have stopped himself yelling as soon as he walked in the door when he felt the anger rising, the situation could have been reversed – so easy to say, so difficult to do on the spur of the moment. However, for us, self-reflecting and recognising the opportunity for change, reactivity will be brought into check.

Let's continue to look at what is going on for Dad. His 3Ss had been triggered earlier in the day when his boss was dissatisfied with his work. As he walked in the door and saw the disorder in his home it unconsciously amplified his distress. When he was a child disorder in the house signalled the beginning of his parents' relationship breakdown. His mother was a 'neat freak' and when she became demotivated with her marriage she lost her impetus to keep the house ordered.

Gradually we start to see how all the little pieces add up to create a mosaic of emotions and triggers in our relationships.

Ideally Dad could have recognised the distress he was feeling and said to himself 'I am feeling a little vulnerable at the moment, I will be gentle with myself and reassure myself that things will be OK'. For her part Mum could have recognised the feeling of being criticised as being a trigger from her childhood and been less defensive. Later Dad may have worked out why his boss criticising his work worried him and would be in a better position to deal with the situation at work.

Quick recap: our projections onto others influence the way we think about them, which in turn impacts our behaviour and, like a chain reaction, then influences their behaviour towards us.

The Neuroscience

From a neuroscience standpoint we will always see situations through the lens of our own experience. We cannot fail because our experience and behaviour has encoded our brain through the firing of neurons. Experiences shape neuronal connection through our memory. Thus encoding acts "as a kind of funnel,"[26] says Siegel, which we use to help us anticipate what is to come and prepare us for action.

The downside of seeing situations through the lens of our own experience is that this lens was formed out of conscious awareness, which unconsciously biases our perceptions and our view of reality. This subsequently impacts on how we engage with the world around us. It is frightening to realise that our programming is all happening out of our conscious awareness. An analogy may be someone altering the hard drive of your computer while you were out and you have no idea it's happened.

We know that ongoing experience continues to shape the brain throughout our life by altering the connections among neurons. As Siegel[27] says: "neural firing (experience) allows the brain to change its internal connections (memory). Experience shapes the

---

[26] Dr Dan Siegel, *The Developing Mind.*
[27] Dr Dan Siegel, *Pocket Guide to Interpersonal Neurobiology.*

brain and this process goes on throughout life ... we also know that the mind develops as the genetically programmed maturation of the brain responds to ongoing experience." The interesting aspect is that while your interpretation of what you perceive is shaped by what you have experienced your perception shapes how you process what you experience. We have the ability to question and change our perceptions. This capacity to change perception is what gives us flexibility and brain plasticity.

It might not be us at all but them!

So far this has all been about us, but it is helpful to consider how all this information relates to other people. When others become reactive to us and we can't understand why, consider that maybe we are triggering something in their unconscious, which has **nothing** to do with us.

Others have their own programming and often, unbeknown to us, some aspect of our behaviour or mannerisms may, at an unconscious level, remind them of someone else. Their association with that previous experience may have been unhappy and it triggered their crocodile into feeling aggressive or defensive. Conversely, it may have been a productive association, where someone was overly giving or attentive, and they unconsciously expect the same from us, which may be more than we are prepared or able to give.

Maria is a kindly middle-aged boss who has been in her role for many years and genuinely wants the best for her employees. But Cherie, a new employee, is demanding. Maria knows she has had personal problems with the recent death of her mother and her loneliness so goes out of her way to help her. However Maria finds that the more she tries to help the less initiative Cherie shows. As Maria's frustration grows she gives Cherie a first warning. Cherie gets reactive and aggressive and hands in her resignation. Maria feels particularly frustrated that she has wasted so much time and energy on an employee who has not stayed and she will have to start her search for a new person.

What could Maria have done differently? She probably could not have realised that Cherie was projecting a mother figure onto her but as she started to feel her frustration grow she could have talked to Cherie to tell her she had to use her own initiative rather than running to her. Ideally Maria could have put firmer boundaries in place much earlier, however she was unconsciously filling her own need to be caring. At some level she missed her mothering role.

Others are at the centre of their own universes; it is not all about us

When others become reactive and we can't understand why, it is helpful to stop and reflect. Others' anger either fuels our own anger or our defensiveness. This is a natural reaction and stems straight from our crocodile brain. It is important to take a step back before we react emotionally and expend precious energy, because it may not be about us at all.

When this situation arises in your relationships, check in with the other person to see if our actions have impacted them in some way. Ask questions such as: I feel something is going on for you, is it anything I have done or said? Or: I am concerned that I may have upset you in some way – is that the case?

We are so used to being the centre of our own universe we can find it extremely difficult to imagine that it is not about us at all. It is about the other.

Taking Responsibility

At the end of the day, whether we like it or not, we are responsible for the choices and actions we take. You may be ordered to do something but ultimately you are responsible for the doing. No one can get into our head and physically manipulate or control our feelings. Responsibility for our relationships begins and ends with us. We choose how we relate to everyone and everything in our life. We run our own control centre.

Sounds heavy doesn't it? The good news is that as we train ourselves to become aware we are changing our brain. We are using its plasticity to grow new neural connections and rewiring it for more positive behaviours, which sets us up for further successful interactions and rewarding relationships.

In the past our programming would have dominated the choices we made, but that was then and this is now. Now we are in a different place of awareness, a new state that behoves us to reflect carefully when we catch ourselves resorting, for instance, to the old instinctive behaviour of blaming others for the situation we are in.

It is difficult to take responsibility because we would prefer not to look at the part we play in our interpersonal relationships and circumstances, particularly when things are not working out the way we want. We don't want to admit our faults or own up to the part we have played. It is much easier to either become emotionally reactive or emotionally cut off than take responsibility. And we could blame our crocodile brain for that.

Responsibility means not demanding others to change their behaviour so we feel better

Responsibility means not demanding others to change so that we feel less anxious, frustrated, upset, depressed, angry or victimised or whatever the emotion is. Responsibility is recognising what we are feeling and taking control of our emotions, not projecting them onto others.

> *Blake is a student enrolled in a course beyond his capability. Struggling, he complains the teaching is poor. It was easier to find fault and blame the teaching than to take responsibility for his part in choosing a course that was beyond his capability. He projected his own frustration by blaming the teacher.*

Translating Blake's example into the work environment, most of the time we would rather change jobs than admit culpability for our part in a difficult dynamic with our boss or our peers. We often project onto them accusing, them of being difficult. And indeed they may be difficult, and usually are, but we have a part to play in this dynamic and we are also choosing to see them as difficult rather than think creatively about the situation. What can I learn to do differently? How can I look at this situation another way?

Remember each time we do something different we are establishing new neural connections improving our brain functioning.

Chapter Recap

Our projections influence the way we think about others and that in turn affects our behaviour. It is a chain reaction.

When we feel emotionally reactive our body is sending us a signal. This is our opportunity to stop and reflect.

Ideally we want to be gentle and compassionate with ourselves when we find ourselves judging others harshly, welcoming the opportunity to learn about our secret self and our reactive, instinctive crocodile brain, rather than trying to avoid or deny what we are feeling.

In the same way others trigger us and our programming we may be triggering them. Often this is at an unconscious level and it's not about us at all. If we can check out with them what is happening the relationship will grow.

We are ALL 100% responsible for the thoughts and actions we take.

We run our own control centre. No one else can get into our head and physically manipulate or control our feelings so responsibility for all our relationships begins and ends with us. We choose how we relate to everyone and everything in our life.

The good news is that each and every time we look at a situation differently we begin to rewire and improve our brain function.

Your journey

Think of a situation that impacted you in your personal life and how that affected how you interacted with others and your performance at work. How do you think others could have been influenced by your mood?

Think of someone you have found difficult in the work environment and reflect on what might have happened, or been happening, in their personal life and how that might be impacting their behaviour towards you.

Chapter 9

What does this mean for business?

The extraordinary scientist Albert Einstein told us "you cannot solve problems at the same level of consciousness that created them". And that is why it is important we learn different strategies if we want business and relationships to function well.

At the risk of sounding trite and somewhat negative we know that organisations are the product of the actions and behaviour of the individuals employed. What impacts the individual impacts the organisation. Organisational awareness of the 7 keys helps prevent disruptive behaviour, increasing productivity and teamwork.

Unless management has some understanding of how employees unconsciously react – expect the social system to take precedence over the corporate system, (chapter 1,) as well as employees' unconscious expectation that business will look after them in a similar way to Mum and Dad – trouble can and often does raise its ugly head, leading to frustration and often anger from both sides. The following dynamic is easily recognised.

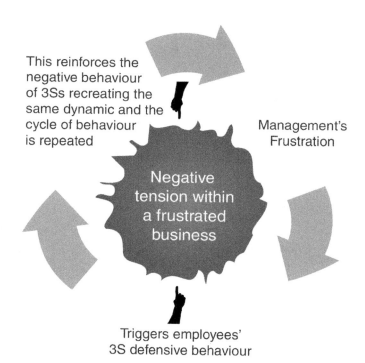

Dynamic That Often
Operates In Business

This reinforces the
negative behaviour
of 3Ss recreating the
same dynamic and the
cycle of behaviour
is repeated

Management's
Frustration

Negative
tension within
a frustrated
business

Triggers employees'
3S defensive behaviour

can advance to their full potential when the 3Ss are
threatened, because, as seen overleaf, when survival

139

mechanisms kick in effective listening goes out of the door and so does effective management.

We know that increased reactivity leads to decreased profitability as a result of the ensuing politics, loss of focus, diversionary tactics, distrust, confusion, demoralisation, gossip, inefficiency, rigidity, deception, withholding of information etc, and the list goes on.

While it almost certainly not what management wants to hear, it is essential to recognise that employees' histories are often the unconscious drivers of the organisation. To avoid being held down in the lower levels of social/political conflict zones it is important to be aware that until each individual becomes aware and conscious, organisations generally will be held back by unconscious, rigid, inflexible thought patterns of everyone, from the Board down.

We are all guilty of this at times and have thoughts and beliefs that are out of conscious awareness until we do this work.

This major problem is then overlaid by the hierarchical system we talked of earlier. Our crocodile brains are unconsciously triggered by the power differentials that operate in a hierarchical system. Management is seen as the 'big people', says Margot Cairnes, thought leader and change agent, in her book, *Approaching the Corporate Heart.*[28] The unconscious projection from employees is that big people are surrogate parents. This belief system diminishes individuals' choice and the taking of responsibility. We, as employees, unconsciously often think of the workplace as unsafe, because we could be judged negatively.

---

[28] Margot Cairnes, *Approaching the Corporate Heart.*

141

Management takes on the projection of surrogate parents

Management, again unconsciously, will usually take on this projection of being surrogate parents and try to fulfil the role. This usually involves micro-managing, as the general assumption is that employees are incapable unless they are continually being supervised and instructed.

The downside of this is that we are robbed of personal power as management takes on the quasi role of parent and employees readily accept this. A feedback loop forms that is a powerful negative dynamic and hard to break. The lack of autonomy goes up the line as management is aware of senior management judging their performance. And the same occurs at Board level. If it is a public company both shareholders and the press are judging the company's performance.

The good news is that once management and employees are aware of this dynamic and how it has evolved its impact can be reduced. Empowered employees have awareness of their thoughts and actions, which maximises their own and the organisation's potential. As we know, to raise our level of awareness we need to become conscious of the power of our unconscious and the underlying motivations behind our thoughts and actions. Becoming responsible for our thoughts and actions we maximise our potential to be flexible, innovative and creative. Education as well as self-monitoring enables us to become empowered, valuable employees who are not reacting out of a defensive 3S state.

It is increasingly important for employees to recognise that the organisation has a hierarchy of needs to be met in order for their jobs to be secure and to create the arena for their own potential to be realised.

When we have awareness of both corporate and social systems we can move forward to new heights. This has a valuable competitive advantage. Interdependence between management and employees is essential to operate at higher levels. Enlightened team members can build truly successful teams. Enlightened team members are aware, conscious of their own thinking, and understand that the organisation provides them with an arena to be the best they can be. Without the arena or the stage to play on, how can we have choice about how to behave in any particular work situation?

Employees are the life blood of any company and if the small-time stuff such as overbearing authoritarian attitudes and childish behaviour can be addressed by giving people the opportunity to understand where their thinking originates, the creative energy released will be substantial.

Companies breaking the 3S cycle will enable flexibility, adaptability, creativity, trust, health and enthusiasm in their employees. The trust that will be built will be based on mutual benefit for both the organisation and the individual.

Bringing all of who we are to our careers

To work successfully within a complex market we need to bring the whole of who we are to our careers. Today's complex problems can no longer be solved by old solutions. In a tough market environment solving difficult issues needs more than shared ideas. Solutions have to emerge through "a creative generative process ..." says Kahane,[29] an international consultant and author helping business with change. "The authoritarian pattern of talking is that bosses and experts talk down – dictating and telling – and everyone else talks cautiously. This is the closed way. To solve complex problems, it is important to find a more open way."[30] Our Gen Ys are more diverse and increasingly more able to talk up to change the old dynamic. Members of the older generation sometimes find this disrespectful, but that is our perception coming from earlier programming of 'respect your elders'.

We cannot develop creative solutions to complex situations unless we can hear, see and open up to include the whole of who we are, our feelings, our personality, our history and our desires. Complexity theory – remember the theory of complexity we looked at in the first chapter, when a system is allowed to move towards complexity, with individuals differentiated, (separate yet linked). With differentiation the organisation can operate as a functional whole. This means increasing complex interactions between individuals with all employees taking responsibility and moving towards self-actualisation. Organisations then operate at higher levels.

---

[29] Adam Kahane, *Solving Tough Problems*.
[30] Adam Kahane, *Solving Tough Problems*.

Being open

Part of the new paradigm is to be open, which can feel vulnerable; however, paradoxically, that vulnerability is our greatest strength. The open way is for people to become real, honest, and more authentic which brings greater energy with it. Our authentic self comes from a place of personal truth. Ideally we lift the mask when we walk into the office. We are human, working together to advance our company, our country, our planet and ourselves. By working at higher levels each of us share these common aspirations.

It is our fear of being thought inadequate and vulnerable in some way that gets in the way of being open and bringing all of ourselves to our workplace. Openness means that our ideas can be challenged and rejected. They can even be thought of as stupid, which no doubt is what many of us heard throughout our childhood and at some level have probably absorbed as truth.

Fear of being considered incompetent is an almost universally held belief. Fear of foolishness closes us down and we assume others, particularly our bosses, know better. This cycle self-perpetuates, increasing the belief of inadequacy and locks us into fear – back to the 3Ss. If we can override our own fear and reveal our ideas we give others permission to come up with other ideas. They may not always be appropriate yet often, seed creativity. Perhaps more importantly disclosure will bring closeness and team spirit, giving rise to fertile ground for implementation of solutions and ideas.

Working at a higher level of consciousness

When managers take responsibility for instigating different behaviour it has an automatic flow-on effect to the rest of the organisation. This is because when one part of a system changes the whole system has to change. Imagine a clock, when one part doesn't work properly the clock can't function efficiently. The same applies to a car or any other system.

As humans, when we take responsibility and are aware we become more respectful of others and this helps to break the damaging 3S cycle. We can start to work at a higher level of consciousness and the system works more cohesively and comfortably. The synergies flow and together we become greater than the sum of our parts. Furthermore as people see us change little by little they change too. Whilst we can't change others (once they are no longer children) we can be role models by being respectful and responsible. We can support change by modelling it.

As organisational synergies flow, people, (customers and competition) see the organisation change and it helps them have the courage to change their own organisations, leading to a more fulfilling business environment.

We reinvent and renew ourselves when we operate with intent, consciousness, authenticity and attention. Working with intention in a more fully conscious respectful way brings harmony and authenticity.

Scharmer[31] (Massachusetts Institute of Technology Sloan School of Management) says that when attention is given, energy follows and decisions can be taken easily and quickly. He talks about the emerging field as we truly listen to each other, which will enable us to learn from the future as it emerges. There is an emerging science of renewing and reinventing ourselves through bringing consciousness and attention to bear.

Chapter Recap

Businesses are the product of the actions and behaviour of the individuals employed. What impacts the individual impacts the business.

Managers are more effective when they have some understanding of how employees unconsciously react in order to manage expectations on both sides.

If the 3Ss are activated there is no effective management as internal politics reign and the system becomes inefficient.

Employees' histories are often the unconscious drivers of the organisation.

Hierarchical system activates employees' expectations that management acts as surrogate parents, reducing creativity and productivity.

It is important we become responsible for our thoughts and actions to maximise our potential.

---

[31] Dr Otto Scharmer, *Theory U, Leading from the future as it emerges*, 2007.

When the reactive cycle of the 3Ss is reduced by education and understanding, both organisation and employees, can strive for their full potential raising the level of consciousness.

We reinvent and renew ourselves when we operate with intent, consciousness, authenticity and attention.

Your journey

Can you see how you might become more differentiated at work, either in your interactions with people that report to you or how you respond in your role?

Can you see areas where the hierarchical system could be modified? What would that new structure look like?

Chapter 10

Empowerment – 7 keys into 3 main points, awareness, choice and responsibility

Before we turn to business let's take a moment to look at the personal journey you have undertaken here. It's challenging being responsible, honest, authentic and conscious. It takes courage, continual self-monitoring and discipline. However we reinvent and renew ourselves when we operate with intent, consciousness, authenticity and attention, says Scharmer.[32] He has a "simple assumption: every human is not one but two. One is the person who we have become through the journey of the past. The other one is the dormant being of the future we could become through our forward journey. Who we become will depend on the choices we make and the actions we take now."

For the most part becoming conscious, responsible and authentic, disables old ingrained behaviour patterns, learnt as small children to avoid trouble when we felt helpless and powerless. After all, even Adam and Eve avoided responsibility by blaming the serpent!

We know that understanding where our behaviour comes from makes it easier to make appropriate changes. The good news is that when we become conscious and take responsibility we change our interpersonal dynamics. We are firmly in the driver's

---

[32] Dr Otto Scharmer, *Theory U, Leading from the future as it emerges*, 2007.

seat of our own car, we become empowered and can make rational choices for our highest good. This substantially reduces our stress levels, our reactivity to others [and increases our overall happiness], all major contributors to relationship success.

Professor Fred Kofman in his book *Conscious Business*[33] talks about the dignity we have when we decide how we want to behave in any given situation. He says we have choice in the way we want to respond and we can choose to ennoble ourselves by the choices we make, as our attitude is the full expression of who we are. We have unconditional responsibility in choosing how we want to be.

What's more, when we become conscious and take responsibility for our behaviour it has an automatic flow-on to others.

A quick recap of what we have gained from the **7 keys to Successful Relationships** put in a different way:

---

[33] Dr Fred Kofman, *Conscious Business.*

How it all fits together

Brain: 3 levels of the brain

- Crocodile (manifests through the unconscious)
- Horse (manifests through the unconscious)
- Neo-cortex

Unconscious:

- What it does, how it works
- How it is programmed
- What happens when it feels threatened

Beliefs:

- Initially stem from programming of the unconscious by parents
- Rarely change in a lifetime unless beliefs are re-examined
- Largely accepted as the status quo

Secret Self:

- Secret self – represses so-called unattractive qualities
- Not acknowledged, nevertheless very human

Projection:

- The secret self's weapon
- The things we dislike or don't acknowledge in ourselves we see in others and become our triggers
- These triggers tell us about our unconscious beliefs and motivations

The Relationship

- Continually impacted by our projections and beliefs about how others should behave, which are largely unconscious
- All the repressed and suppressed energy from our secret self and our beliefs find a home in others!
- Our personal triggers impact others, mainly negatively
- RESULTS DISASTROUS

Solution

- Understand your unconscious programming
- Take responsibility
- RELATIONSHIPS FLOURISH

Although we have not yet covered the solution in detail essentially it is to **take responsibility**. Before going there we have:

- Awareness of where our behaviour originated

- An understanding of our programming and some of our personal drivers

- We know our programming manifests itself in our secret self and then in our behaviours

- We know we have a point of choice in how to behave in each and every interaction, without our unconscious making a quick almost automatic decision out of our awareness

- We know that when we have problems in our interpersonal relationships that it is often more about us and our programming than it is about other people

- With awareness we enable a more informed choice of action

- With this understanding we in turn realise that others may be unconsciously reacting out of their own programming and it may not have anything to do with us, which gives us the opportunity to defuse a potential conflict or not be as affected as we might once have been

At the risk of sounding repetitive it is important to distil these seven principles into three key points:

- Awareness of where our behaviour comes from

- That awareness now gives us choice in how we behave in each and every interaction

- We recognise our responsibility for our part in any interpersonal dynamic

Let's spend a few minutes thinking about how our own personal responsibility impacts on the business we work for. We know that highly successful people are self-motivated and self-managed. In short, they are disciplined and responsible, as well as wanting the best for both themselves and their organisation. They do not blame circumstances and other people; they work hard to find their way around difficulties. They do not need to be tightly managed because they are already self-starters. They know the difference between completing a task list just to get a job done and the drive and responsibility to do the job in the best possible way. They fulfil commitments when they say they will in a culture of responsibility and discipline. They know it takes continual discipline, self-monitoring and determined courage in order to achieve. They also have the passion to be the best that they can be, both personally and in their business environment.

In a business arena we know that the primary ingredient to build an exceptional organisation is its people. They must have the qualities mentioned above in order to drive the organisation to exceptional success. The trick for leaders is how to achieve this, because it has to come from the top. Business is a collection of people and what takes it forward is hiring the appropriate people and keeping them motivated to be the best they can be.

When you as a leader understand yourself better you will automatically understand and appreciate the dilemmas that face those working for you. You will read people more easily, which makes the task of motivating them easier. You will be able to guide them respectfully and assertively, without undue frustration in most cases. There will be exceptions and after giving them a fair opportunity for change you will need to be clear and firm. If they don't espouse the same values as you and your organisation you have probably made a mistake in hiring them. They have to want to serve the organisation as well as themselves.

If you as management have to put in rigid rules and processes in order to keep your business profitable you will drive away the self-starter, self-motivator, says respected business author Jim Collins.[34] They will not want to work in a rigid environment. Again coming back to the theory of complexity, it enables business to be its most flexible, adaptable and stable. In today's world that is what we need.

Rigidity means mediocrity

Rigidity turns businesses into bureaucracy, which often means mediocrity. Gen Y, (1981 – 1994) our future leaders, are very much the generation who don't want to fit into the norms of the more conservative older generations. They have been born into an age of huge technological change and they are used to having a voice, which often gets stifled in a bureaucracy. They are a generation of self-starters that believe they can get what they want and tend not to stay in organisations that are not flexible and adaptable. They embrace change and will be our creative leaders propelling business forward. But we have to create the arena to facilitate opportunity and creativity.

What we are currently seeing in the Australian business scene is the exit or severe profit deterioration of some very large companies. A large part of this is due to the fact that workers are operating under the social system (needing their own needs met) rather than in conjunction with the corporate system (product-orientated).

---

[34] Tim Collins, *How the Mighty Fall.*

Unless workers can modify their expectations and also change with the global situation many will invariably lose their jobs, as industry has to close unprofitable operations to stay afloat. We are in a period of massive change, happening very fast, and management has to be clear about what is needed to keep up with the change. If the people can't change because they are still operating in their own personal rigid framework, expecting business to be surrogate mothers and fathers, they will drag the company down and they are not right for your organisation.

Coming back to the seven core principles, ultimately we all need to be responsible for the choices we make. Usually change doesn't happen without pain. Coming back to what we have learnt by looking at both the psychology and neuroscience of how our brain works, we know that it is both remarkably primitive and sophisticated at the same time. Our brain is primed to look after itself and ensure survival, but it takes huge brain energy/effort to stop reacting, become more conscious and take responsibility. We know survival is hard-wired and its default patterns are firmly entrenched but when we can fully grasp the principles above it becomes so much easier to manage both our team and ourselves. While we are trying to be the best we can be we have a brain that wants to dominate in the way it thinks best, and we need to harness its ability and use all of our attributes – we need to harness our crocodile and our horse or mammalian brain – and be firmly in the saddle directing our lives.

We know that the brain changes when we focus, says famous psychiatrist and researcher Dr Norman Doidge in his wonderful book, *The Brain That Changes Itself*.[35] Attention changes the brain if we pay enough attention to stimuli, but it is often difficult to direct that attention for long enough. The key is to hold the focus so new neural circuits grow and develop. As we focus on what is happening to us emotionally, become more aware and then self-reflect. Over time, doing this regularly, we are lifting and enhancing our level of conscious. We are becoming more conscious. This focused self-reflection, which as a conscious process can deepen self-understanding, Siegel[36] says and "may be a way to alter mental models and open the door to ongoing development throughout life". Taking time to reflect opens the door to conscious awareness bringing change. Or as Scharmer paraphrasing Bill O'Brien, the late CEO of Hanover Insurance, says: "the success of our actions as change-makers does not depend on *what we do or how we do it* but on *the inner place* from which we operate".[37]

All of this leads us to a whole new level of consciousness and enables us to reach our fullest potential in every way.

We have gained a new level of empowerment and the more we can act on these key understandings the greater our impact. Everything gets easier – our lives, our relationships, our work and finally our world.

---

[35] Dr Norman Doidge, *The Brain that changes itself*.
[36] Dr Dan Siegel, *Mindsight*.
[37] Scharmer and Kaufer, *Leading from the Emerging Future: From Ego-System to Eco-System Economies*, 2013.

The greatest gift we can give ourselves and the planet

An Indian holy man once said that the greatest gift we can give the planet is a healthy you. This is undoubtedly true.

So what is psychological health? Psychological health is an integration of yourself, acknowledging and embracing your secret self, an ability to take responsibility for yourself and your actions, communicating honestly with yourself and others, being aware of your projections, and having a strong belief and respect for yourself.

When we can do all that we are psychologically healthy and we know that our brain is changing accordingly – our flexibility translates as brain plasticity.

We can stand in our own integrity, aware of our needs, whilst being aware of how much we can ask of others. We are able to hold the tensions of competing demands and conflicting ideas with composure, knowing that we are trying to do the best we can. What a gift to the world.

As a rule when we are psychologically healthy, our biology follows suite. The neuroscience tells us that every time we feel an emotion our brain sends a chemical flush of hormones through our body.

If those emotions are negative our body will receive a quick flush of cortisol (stress hormone), which as you can imagine is not good if it is happening a lot of the time. While we are becoming more and more aware we are able to control those negative chemical flushes and as we train our brains we are also changing our bodies. At the same time the flow-on is a better world with happier relationships.

The greatest gift you can give yourself is an unconditional belief in yourself, and the greatest gift you can give the world is to become self-aware and take responsibility for your feelings and actions.

"Enlightenment is taking responsibility for your actions," says Wayne Dyer [37]. Dyer is the internationally renowned author and speaker in self-development.

We are humans working together to advance ourselves, our family, our company, our country and our planet. By working at higher levels each of us share these common aspirations.

Your greatest gift to humanity, is a healthy you. In becoming aware we know if we are operating out of love or fear. It really does come down to being that simple. A useful question to ask is, am I doing this out of love or fear? In a business context the word love may not sound appropriate, so we could replace it with respect for both yourself and others, which is essentially what love is. When we transcend the fear and our unconscious reactions (3Ss) and choose to operate out of a paradigm of respect we are magnificently empowered.

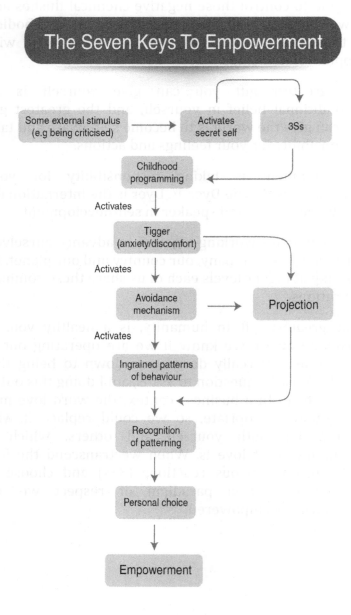

The Seven Keys To Empowerment

Some external stimulus (e.g being criticised) → Activates secret self | 3Ss

Childhood programming

Activates

Tigger (anxiety/discomfort)

Activates

Avoidance mechanism → Projection

Activates

Ingrained patterns of behaviour

Recognition of patterning

Personal choice

Empowerment

- 3 levels of the brain
- Crocodile (manifests through unconcious)
- Horse (manifests through unconscious)
- Neo-cortex

- Unconcious - What it does, how it works
- How it is programmed
- What happens when it feels threatened

- Secret self - repressed so-called unattractive qualities
- Not acknowledged, nevertheless very human

- Initially stem from programming of the unconscious by parents
- Rarely change in a lifetime unless beliefs are uncovered and examined
- Largely accepted as the status quo

- The secret self's weapon
- The things we dislike or don't acknowledge in ourselves we see in others
- Become our triggers
- Tell us about our unconcious beliefs and motivations

- Continually impacted by our projections and beliefs about how others should behave, which are largely unconscious
- All the repressed and the suppressed energy from our secret self and our beliefs find a home in others!
- Our personal triggers impact others, mainly negatively
- RESULT DISASTROUS

- Undestand your unconcious programming
- Take responsibility
- RELATIONSHIPS FLOURISH

Lightning Source UK Ltd.
Milton Keynes UK
UKOW06f1112050617

302709UK00001B/195/P